sex toys
101
A PLAYFULLY UNINHIBITED GUIDE

RACHEL VENNING & CLAIRE CAVANAH
Founders of Toys in Babeland

A FIRESIDE BOOK
Published by Simon & Schuster
New York • London • Toronto • Sydney • Singapore

FIRESIDE
Rockefeller Center
1230 Avenue of the Americas
New York, NY 10020

FIRESIDE and colophon are registered trademarks
of Simon & Schuster, Inc.

Toys in Babeland and Sex Toys 101 are registered trademarks of Toys in Babeland, LLC.

For information about special discounts for bulk purchases,
please contact Simon & Schuster Special Sales:
1-800-456-6798
or business@simonandschuster.com.

A Quirk Packaging Book
Designed by Lynne Yeamans
Photography by Hotfoot Studio
Illustrations © Fish

Manufactured in Singapore

10 9 8 7 6 5 4 3 2 1

Library of Congress Cataloging-in-Publication Data is available.

ISBN 0-7432-4351-X

Sex can be a risky activity; not as risky as ski jumping, but more risky than channel surfing. Please use common sense when playing with sex toys—for example, turn the power button off when a toy is not in use, examine toys for rough edges before inserting into any orifices, check the batteries, and be careful with bondage equipment. Most importantly, follow manufacturers' or other directions that come with your toys. We do not manufacture any of the toys in this book, and make no warranties about them or their safe use. Our recommendations are based on likes and dislikes, not product liability. We'd be happy to take partial credit for the joy that learning about sex toys may bring you, but we disclaim any responsibility for any damage caused, or alleged to be caused, directly or indirectly, by the information or the lack of information provided in this book.

We dedicate this book to the Babes of Toys in Babeland.

ACKNOWLEDGMENTS

Toys in Babeland owes its existence to certain people and movements. In the 1980s, when there was a confluence of the gay rights movement and the feminist movement (both inspired by liberation movements of the 1960s) we were lucky enough to be in college, among the first generation of students who had teachers and communities that encouraged us to think and talk about sex. Thank you to everyone who encouraged our baby steps in sex theory (and practice!) and to everyone whose struggles for the freedom of expression our work is built on.

Opening a store was a big leap into the unknown for us and we could not have done it without tremendous support. Thank you first to Joani Blank for sharing information, offering encouragement, and giving us the belief that it could be done. Thank you to the crew of barnraisers in Seattle and New York who volunteered their time and energy: Chris Andrews, Cathy MacPhail, Monica Mills, Erin Casteel, Amy Jacobsen, Laura Johnson, Anne Hillam, Chichoz Naca, Heather Findlay, Catherine Gund, Nancy Anderson, Ellen Forney, Laura Michalik, Skylar Fein, Sunny Speidel, Holly Morris, the Smellies, Risa Blythe, Kendyll Howard, Erin Healy, Pam Barger, Barbara Marino, Sandy Cioffi, Kelley Scanlon, Liz Randall, Gwen Bialic, Cheryl Perry, Cathie Opie, Murray Hill, Kay Turner, Lynn Comella, Marga Gomez, Anne D'Adesky, and all of the first brave customers.

Over the years we've become part of a community dedicated to quality sex toys. Shout outs to retailing and manufacturing pioneers Del Williams, Gosnell Duncan, Trilby Boone, and Kathy Taylor. The toy makers and retailers have been supported by a cadre of sex writers who encourage people to explore their sexuality, including Susie Bright, Carol Queen, Patrick Califia-Rice, Inga Muscio, Tristan Taormino, Dan Savage, Karlyn Lotney, Felice Newman and Cleis Press, Dossie Easton, and the Greenery Press writers, along with a number of journalists who write about sex and sexuality. Thanks to all for helping us in our mission. Betty Dodson and Annie Sprinkle inspire with their flamboyant dedication to nurturing sexual development and pleasure.

Thank you to everyone who has worked at Toys in Babeland. You've been our comrades, teachers, and friends.

Thank you to Sharyn Rosart for giving us the opportunity to write this book, and for being so delightful to work with. Thanks also to Lynne Yeamans for bringing the toys to life through her beautiful design. And thank you to Marcela Landres at Simon & Schuster for her enthusiasm about this project.

Rachel: Thanks to my parents for always encouraging me to make my own decisions, even when you didn't like them. And thank you to Laura Weide, for offering me so much love and support, for helping to edit this manuscript, and for sharing your life with me.

Claire: Thank you to my family—to Dad for nurturing my intellectual curiosity, to Kevin for your unconditional love, and to Craig for suggesting we name our store Toys in Babeland. You are a genius. Thank you Candy Halikas for your unswerving personal and professional support and thank you Karen Cook for your encouragement, love, and soft-boiled eggs.

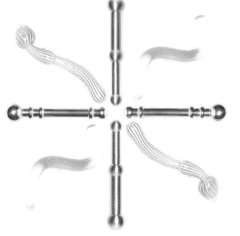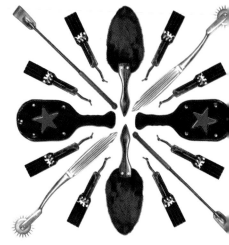
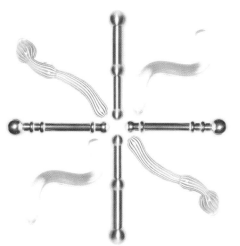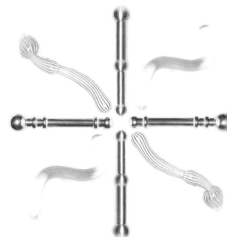
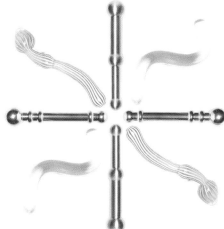

contents

A few years ago, during the annual
Gay Pride Parade, we introduced Brooklyn to
Toys in Babeland's most prized possession—our giant,
velvety pink vulva costume. With our logo pinned on the back
and a Sex Educator inside, the giant vulva pranced down the street
handing out stickers that shout "Polish Your Pearl!" and "Pet Your

introduction:

Bunny!" (euphemisms for female masturbation). Gay Pride is a time to
pull out all the stops—the perfect opportunity to bring Pussy Power
to the outer boroughs. ■ Like Mickey Mouse at Disneyland, the
gigantic vulva was the star of the parade. She shook
hands with politicians, posed for snap-shots
with tourists and charged at

gay men who shrieked in mock horror. One man with a three-year-old child stood on the sidewalk, both of them enjoying the pageant. When the man saw the big pussy approaching, he leaned down and whispered in his child's ear. The little boy smiled broadly, waved to the vulva, and shouted "Hola, Vagina!" ■ Toys in Babeland is out to

toys in babeland

give sex a good name. We're a fun-loving, feminist sex toy store, celebrating sexual vitality and educating our community. Women and vibrators go together like kitties and catnip, yet most places that sell sex toys make women uncomfortable. At Toys in Babeland, we have created an environment where women feel welcome.

While we are careful to make Toys in Babeland a comfortable place for women to shop, our message (and our toys) appeal to men, too. The Sex Educators at Toys in Babeland are like the sex-positive sisters most guys never had. (We call ourselves Sex Educators because we educate people every day as we assist customers.) As cheerleaders for sex toys, we encourage people of all genders and sexualities to pursue their desires, whether those include sex toys or not.

We talk with people about sex every day, and that on-going conversation is the heart of our business. It is the most fun and meaningful part of what we do. There are few spaces in our culture where people can talk about sex openly. In our stores and through our website people get accurate answers to their questions about sex, find out about themselves, and shop for the toys that may help them have new and better sexual experiences.

We created Sex Toys 101, our signature workshop, to present the information we know about sex and sex toys all at once, like a detailed tour of the store for a whole room of people. Through Sex Toys

101 and other workshops, we pick up sex education where discussion of the fallopian tubes and ovaries leaves off. Our workshops have developed into short, powerful consciousness-raising sessions where participants learn about sexual pleasure, and realize they aren't alone in their desire to know more. We share what we know about sexual anatomy, orgasm, and sex toys, and extol the benefits of masturbation, especially for women. As the sex information starts to flow, the room becomes a space where people are free to be honest about their sexual experiences. Camaraderie grows as women who ejaculate find out that it's not urine they are spurting, and pre-orgasmic women share their experiences getting to the "plateau" and no further. The workshops gather people who are opening up to their sexuality, and give them a chance to hear how others experience sex. Everyone seems to feel less alone as they leave, and supported in their search for sexual happiness.

This book grew out of a desire to share that energy and information with more people than those able to take our workshop. Here we offer all the

information we've gathered through the years and serve it up with generous sides of encouragement and advice. We've coupled our text with full-color photographs of some of the toys, in hopes that seeing how good-looking they are will help dispel some of the negative preconceptions about sex toys. Some of them are gorgeous! (Please note that the photos do not show the toys' actual size.) We hope that you'll use this book to get information, inspiration and maybe a laugh or two. We think it's attractive enough to be a "coffee table book;" and hope some of you may be inspired to leave it out in the front room, and share it with your friends. Interesting discussions can get started that way.

If you want more—sex facts, advice, or to see the latest in toys, please visit our website *www.babeland.com*. And you are welcome to contact us directly with reactions to the book, ideas for new toys, or other thoughts: *rachel@babeland.com* and *claire@babeland.com*.

Happiness is what sex is about. Sex toys enhance one of the most playful and liberating parts of our adult lives. For many women, a good vibrator can mean the difference between having orgasms and just wondering about them. For many queer people, dildos and harnesses open a new world of sexual satisfaction and gender expression. Some governments fear sex toys' inherent promise of liberation, and outlaw them. Four states—Texas, Nebraska, Georgia, and Massachusetts—currently have laws on the books restricting the sale of sex toys, and many cities have ordinances that curtail access to these playthings. In Texas, would-be sex toy buyers have to sign a release stating they are purchasing the toy for educational purposes only. It is easier to buy a gun than a vibrator in Texas.

We dream of a sexually liberated citizenry, and by promoting sex toys we hope do a little bit toward bringing about that happy day. We hope this book opens some doors for you, sparks your imagination, or at least answers a question or two. One world, under lube, with vibrators and dildos for all!

Peace and love,

Rachel and Claire

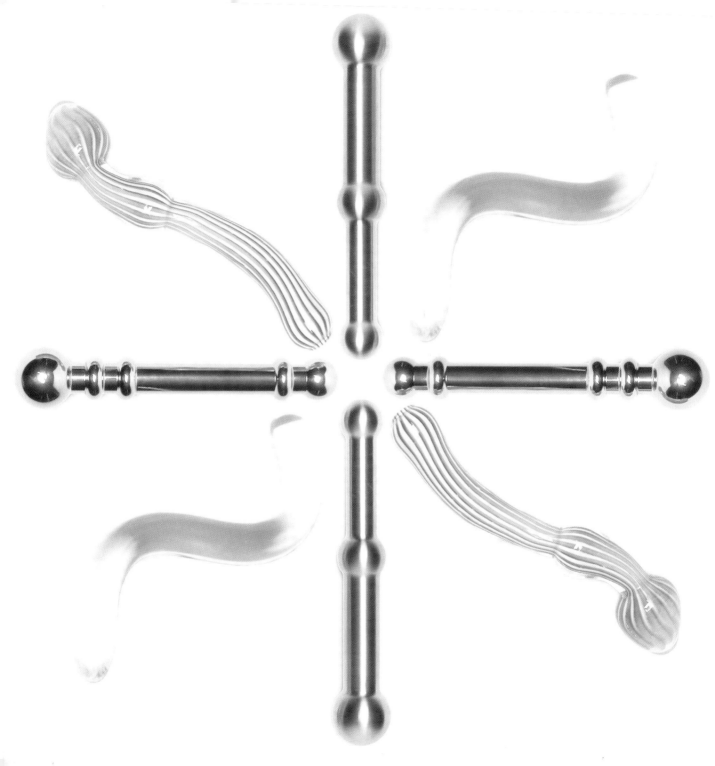

let's play doctor

One memorable fall, Toys in Babeland Sex Educators had a chance to take our G-spotting workshop on the road and into sex-ed history. The carnival-style book release party of a friend of Babeland provided us the opportunity to invite women—and their partners if they had them—to learn about their G-spots hands-on. One Sex Educator played our carnival barker, luring the curious onlookers into our semi-private G-spotting tent. Once they were inside, we gave them more than just a lecture.

sexual anatomy

Up to 10 people could crowd into the tent at one time. One of us would give a cursory explanation of female anatomy, less instruction than they would get at a proper workshop, but more than they ever expected to get at a book release party in a bar. We showed an anatomically correct vulva puppet and a few excellent G-spotting vibrators, then taught them the classic "come here" motion—the curling fingers that so many people use to stroke the G-spot. Then, a Sex Educator snapped on a latex glove, lubed it up, and dropped the bomb: "Okay, who wants to experience it?"

Designed for pleasure: the Kegelcisor, Crystal Wand, Betty's Barbell, and a hand-blown glass dildo.

Jaws dropped open, and there were audible gasps. We didn't know whether anyone would drop her pants or raise her skirts, but the promise of feeling G-spot stimulation doled out by an expert proved too compelling for these seekers to resist. A hand shot up. "We have a taker!" cried the G-spotting expert.

The woman took her place on a chair, and used one of our vibrators to get warmed up. She pulled down her panties. Her boyfriend was looking over our shoulders, focusing on what we were doing as if studying for the most important test of his life. The Sex Educator put two lubed fingers in the student's vagina, searched for the rough spot on the front wall, and gently pushed and rubbed. The woman's body language told the whole story, as her legs parted and her back arched. "What did you just do??" the boyfriend asked, frantic. We explained what to feel for and where. The girlfriend said, "I told you, it's right there!" We gloved the boyfriend and coached him. After the lesson, the couple exited the tent, holding hands, aglow with their new sexual knowledge.

Once the first intrepid woman took our offer, there was no turning back. The line outside our tent snaked around the bar all night.

What's Under the Hood

Knowing sexual anatomy is like having a road map—you might get to your destination if you just start driving and get lucky, but getting where you want to go is a lot more likely if you have a clue to where you're headed. We're going to lay out the map of "down there" with an eye to making sex better; if you understand the mechanics of sexual response, you'll be a better lover to yourself and others.

EXPLORING UNCHARTED TERRITORY

Although sexual images and information seem to be everywhere these days, a lot of people still don't know much about sex. There is a persistent myth that you don't need to seek out knowledge; instead, if you "just do what comes naturally," sex will be deeply satisfying. "Doing what comes naturally" (whatever that is) might work sometimes, but for many people, especially women, that belief leads to a lot of frustration. Learning to reach orgasm is not always easy for women. While some girls do discover their orgasmic capabilities through childhood or adolescent masturbation, many women don't learn to come until they are adults. Learning how to get yourself off is as important for self-sufficiency and emotional intelligence as knowing how to cook a meal or make a friend. In addition to the "sisters are doing it for themselves" factor, women who can't come through masturbation are less likely to reach orgasm with a

So, knowing a thing or two about your body (and the bodies of your lovers) helps ensure against a lifetime of sexual frustration—reason enough to start exploring (if you haven't already). For most men, learning the lay of the genital landscape is pretty simple, and the basic techniques of masturbation come easily. As accomplished masturbators, men move on to partner sex already knowing how to get off. Unfortunately, sometimes men inadvertently train themselves to come quickly—which can lead to adult sexual encounters that are over before they have even begun for the women. On the other hand, our "sex is shameful" culture leaves many women so out of touch with their sexual response that it takes them a long time to come (if they come at all). That sucks!

Sadly, there is still a lot of disapproval of girls and women who explore themselves. Fear of that disapproval, coupled with the fact that female genitals are less visible, means women often are mystified about what's "down there" and how to enjoy it. Sex education offered in schools doesn't do much to clear up the confusion. There are plenty of films about fallopian tubes and descriptions of sexually transmitted diseases, but nothing about sexual pleasure or how to get it.

Sexual desire is a natural part of the human experience, and denying ourselves the pleasure of a deeply satisfying sex life is unnecessary.

partner. But, most of all, the ability to give yourself that pleasure will make you calmer and happier.

Perhaps to compensate for high levels of female sexual frustration, romantic love has long been touted as the ultimate achievement for women. Not to knock being in love, but what happens if that prince or princess never shows up, or if when they get us back to the castle they ignore our clitoris? Sexual desire is a natural part of the human experience, and denying ourselves the pleasure of a deeply satisfying sex life is unnecessary.

Good clean fun: the Sponge Vibe.

Despite the confusion surrounding women's sexual response, a woman's sexual anatomy is no more mysterious than a man's is. In fact, for the first eight weeks of fetal development males and females are indistinguishable. The first stages in the development of the sexual organs are the same. As the fetus develops, male and female sex organs differentiate, but all of the final structures have analogs in both sexes. A little known fact (most doctors and parents keep it hidden) is that a number of people—1or 2 in 2,000—are born intersexed, with genitals that are not clearly male or female, an unsurprising phenomenon considering that the organs start out the same and can go either way depending on which hormones do or do not come into play. It is part of the variation of sexual development. That same variation explains why genitals are like snowflakes, "no two the same."

While women and men have many structural and functional similarities and analogous organs, there are important differences in our sexual road maps. Here is a rundown on the genital basics and how to enjoy them.

What Women Have

When a woman is standing up, not much shows of her genitals but the fur covering the pubic mound and the outer lips and perhaps the inner labia peeking out—unless she has a porn-star shave job, in which case what shows is a lot more skin. To get a good look at herself, a woman must get a mirror, sit down,

spread her legs, and explore. Any woman reading this who hasn't taken a gander, do it now! It's your body, after all—get to know it. Men, if you have a woman lover, ask her to let you take a close look with the lights on. Not only can you learn a thing or two, it's sexy.

At first glance, the clearest features of the genitals are the two sets of lips, inner and outer, the tip of the clitoris, the vagina, and the anus.

Betty's Barbell

It's your body, after all— get to know it.

MEET THE CLITORIS

The tip of the clitoris is the round nub right above the meeting point of the inner labia. It is protected by a little fold of skin, or hood, which is a good thing, because there are 6,000 to 8,000 nerve endings in the clit, and even a light touch is usually extremely intense. As with the penis, the clit is composed of erectile tissue and gets bigger and harder when a woman is turned on. A lot of women prefer their clits touched through the hood, while others enjoy direct touch, usually once they've been warmed up. The clitoris is the only organ in the human body whose sole function is pleasure. How cool is that?

That visible nub of the clit, called the glans, is just the tip of the iceberg. From the exposed tip the shaft continues beneath the skin toward the pubic bone. When a woman is aroused it's easy to feel the shaft beneath the skin—it's a hard inch (2.5cm) or so cylinder of tissue about the width of a straw. After the first inch, it splits into two legs that are similar in

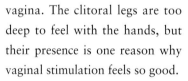

Say "Hey" to the Hymen

Most people know that girls are born with a thin membrane of tissue, called the hymen, which covers or partially covers the vaginal opening. It is usually torn through physical activity or penetration. What you may not know is that sometimes part of the hymen stays intact after the initial tear. Even sexually experienced women may find that a particular position or a larger partner causes discomfort or tearing long after "virginity" is a distant memory. When torn, the hymen often leaves little pieces of membrane inside the vaginal opening. These "hymenal tags" can be sensitive to the touch. (Thanks to Laura Weide for telling us!)

shape to the wishbone of a chicken. These legs curve back beneath the labia toward either side of the vagina. The clitoral legs are too deep to feel with the hands, but their presence is one reason why vaginal stimulation feels so good.

More erectile tissue comes in the shape of two bulbs, nestled just beneath the inner labia between the skin and the clitoral legs. These bulbs reach back to the sides of the vagina. When a woman gets turned on, they swell up with blood

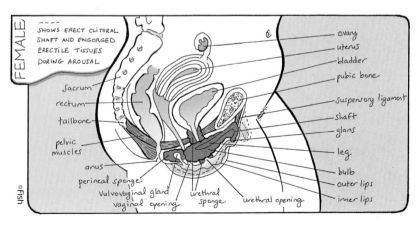

FEMALE

SHOWS ERECT CLITORAL SHAFT AND ENGORGED ERECTILE TISSUES DURING AROUSAL

Sacrum
rectum
tailbone
pelvic muscles
anus
perineal sponge
Vulvovaginal gland
vaginal opening
urethral sponge
urethral opening

ovary
uterus
bladder
pubic bone
suspensory ligament
shaft
glans
leg
bulb
outer lips
inner lips

©Fish

and exert pressure on the clitoral legs and the vaginal walls, and the whole area becomes more sensitive. The entire vulva becomes thicker and swollen as the tissues become engorged—and if you are looking for them, you can see these changes—as visible evidence of arousal.

THE VAGINA

Many people envision the vagina as an open space, waiting to be filled by a penis or sex toy—or as a tubular exit route for babies. In fact it is more like a muscular envelope—the sides touch each other, and separate only when something is inserted. The vagina leads to the cervix, which is the gateway to the female reproductive system. The hole in the cervix (the os) is the only other way in or out, and it is tiny, so there is no danger of losing dildos or other sex toys in the vagina. Most of the nerves are concentrated around the vaginal opening, within the first inch (2.5cm) or two. Between the opening of the vagina and the opening of the anus is a plexus of blood vessels, called the *perineal sponge*, which also becomes engorged and sensitive during arousal. Farther in from the perineum, the wall between the vagina and the anus is quite thin and elastic.

Wondrous Vulva Puppet, by House O' Chicks.

The mucous membrane of the vagina naturally lubricates when excited. The amount and characteristics of this wetness vary a lot depending on several factors, including age, hormonal cycle, diet, stress, and level of hydration. While lubrication can be a good physiological indicator of arousal, its absence doesn't necessarily signal a lack of desire. Natural lube can be supplemented with lube in a bottle. We recommend plenty of water-based lube for penetration, because it lessens the friction that can abrade sensitive tissue. Having to stop fucking because the vaginal opening is sore when the rest of your body still wants it is a bummer.

The majority of nerve endings are around the opening and in the first third of a woman's vagina. Deeper inside there are fewer nerve endings to pick up the subtle sensations of light touch or stroking, but pressure excites the G-spot, and the muscles and ligaments of the region thrill to rhythmic pumping.

When a woman is turned on, penetration often feels so good that all other worries or concerns seem inconsequential compared to the fantastic feelings she experiences. Not only does a good roll in the hay cook up a stew of sex endorphins for her to steep in, but the friction of penetration rightly rubs many of the swollen and sensitive parts we've just described. The G-spot, the bulbs, the perineal sponge, and the clitoral legs are all swollen and pushing against the vaginal walls. Rhythmic, thrusting penetration stimulates all these parts in a pleasurable way. This is great news for the reproduction of the species. As wonderful as penetration often feels, however, it is often not enough to make a woman reach orgasm. Most women need direct, repetitive stimulation on or around the glans of the clit to come. Some positions for intercourse—notably "woman on top," in which she can angle her pelvis just so—allow for more clitoral stimulation. What many women prefer is cunnilingus (that's oral sex), manual stimulation, or a vibrator. Remember: There is no right or wrong way to have an orgasm.

Remember: There is no right or wrong way to have an orgasm.

G-SPOT

The G-spot (or urethral sponge) is among the most misunderstood parts of female sexual anatomy. People mistakenly believe that the G-spot doesn't exist, or that some women have a G-spot and other women don't. Many believe that it takes rare and exacting sexual expertise to find the elusive spot. None of this is true: Every woman has a G-spot, and stimulating it is simple.

Every woman has a G-spot, and stimulating it is simple.

Crystal Wand

"G-spot" is just the name of the spot on the vaginal wall through which the urethral sponge is felt. The urethral sponge is a ring of erectile tissue that surrounds the urethra. It contains glands that when aroused release fluid into the urethra. When a woman is not aroused, the urethral sponge is small and difficult to feel, but if she gets turned on, it swells and is easy to locate. Its rough texture can be felt through the front wall of the vagina (toward the clit). It feels different when aroused, and it's bigger then, so undertake your explorations when turned on. Just use your finger(s) to feel for an area a couple of inches in that resembles the surface of a spongy walnut. Fingers crooked in a "come hither" shape are best angled to find the G-spot. The urethral sponge is behind the vaginal wall, so press firmly— light stroking won't do much. A "pulling" rather than a "poking" motion is usually more arousing. If a woman is really turned on, and the G-spot is swollen, and she bears down hard, it's sometimes possible to see it peeking out from the vaginal opening. Whether you can feel it, see it, or not, every woman has one. To some it's not much of an erogenous zone, but to others it's right up there with the mouth, the clit, and the mind.

Some women ejaculate from G-spot stimulation. That can be a pretty surprising experience if you aren't expecting it. The volume of fluid that spurts out of the urethra can vary from a few drops to a copious amount. If you feel as if you're going to pee while having sex, it's likely that it's female ejaculation, not urine. Pee before penetration so that your bladder is empty, and then if you have that feeling, just let it happen. Worst case is, you peed, but it's more likely that you squirted ejaculate. You've given yourself permission to let go more completely. A simple sniff test will let you know whether it's pee or not. Some women with strong vaginal muscles can ejaculate without direct G-spot stimulation. The rhythmic squeezing of their powerful pubococcygeus (PC) muscles during orgasm provides sufficient stimulation to squirt.

G-spots respond to firm rhythmic touch. It's easiest to reach the G-spot with a slightly curved device, such as arched fingers or a curved dildo designed for G-spot use. Penises and other straight objects can also get to the G-spot, depending on the position or angle of penetration. The G-spot can be felt through the front wall of the vagina, so aim for that area if G-spot stimulation is your goal. Remember that it's not about "poke, poke, poke." A pulling or dragging sensation is what feels best.

Unfortunately, science hasn't determined precisely what female ejaculate is. The

Archer Wand

tissue that develops into the prostate in male fetuses becomes the urethral sponge in females. The prostate makes seminal fluid (only sperm comes from the testicles), so it seems reasonable to determine that female ejaculate is analogous to seminal fluid. It also appears that the fluid is created through sexual arousal, rather than being stored up over time and released. It's similar to sweat in that way. For more info on the G-spot and female ejaculation, check out the book *The Clitoral Truth* by Rebecca Chalker; it's got a wonderful chapter dedicated to demystifying this important aspect of female sexual response. More research on this underexplored area needs to be done, so if you're a doctor or scientist looking for a research project, please take this one on!

WE ♥ ASSHOLES

Women enjoy anal sex because it feels good in a unique way. The external anal area has lots of nerve endings, and it feels fantastic to be stroked and massaged in this area. Spanking, kneading, stroking, and squeezing the cheeks are nice, and anal licking feels so good that it has its own name: rimming. Many people thrill to the sensation of the anal sphincters opening and closing around anal beads or other toys, and because the wall between the anus and vagina is so thin, it's possible to get G-spot stimulation through the back door. Additionally, some women enjoy the feeling of fullness that comes from wearing a butt plug.

Our culture has a strong anal taboo, and a lot of us hold a significant amount of anal tension at all times, especially when nervous. We're literally a society of tight asses. People fear that if they have anal sex, they'll lose their anal tension, and consequently will lose control over their bowels. That's just wrong. In fact, all that extra clenching is unhealthy, and can lead to hemorrhoids and elimination problems. Anal pleasure and health go together, not anal tension and health. Focusing awareness on the anal area, learning to relax the sphincters and feel subtle sensations in the asshole, increases anal well-being. Pleasurable

> Spanking, kneading, stroking, and squeezing the cheeks are nice, and anal licking feels so good that it has its own name: rimming.

anal sex helps folks develop a better sense of connection to (as opposed to alienation from) their assholes, and the stretching and relaxing required for penetration can improve the tone of anal muscles. All that awareness and relaxation also helps prevent stress-related anal maladies, expands the realm of sexual response, and broadens the range of orgasms. Anal sex is like yoga for the butt—it becomes more toned and feels great.

From the pleasing pucker of the anal opening the anus continues on about one inch (2.5cm) to a second sphincter, and beyond that lies the rectum, which is anywhere from 5 to 9 inches (12.5–22cm) long.

The outer sphincter is a voluntary muscle, meaning we can consciously relax it, while the inner is involuntary, meaning it responds to our autonomic nervous system. Because the sphincters work in tandem, learning to relax the outer sphincter helps relax the inner sphincter as well. The rectum is curved in a gentle S shape and is normally empty. In a healthy digestive system, poop moves from the colon into the rectum, where it knocks on the door of the inner sphincter. That sphincter says "Okay," but the voluntary sphincter says, "Wait, I have to find a bathroom." We do, and after we move our bowels, the rectum is empty again. That empty rectum is as far as beads, plugs, fingers, or penises go.

It's reassuring to know that anal sex does not necessarily mean contact with fecal matter. To borrow a phrase, "Shit happens." A trace of poop may be the price of all the fun of anal sex, but it isn't anything a little soap and water won't wash away. To be more confident of one's cleanliness, wash carefully in the shower before sex and, if desired, use a small warm-water anal douche to rinse out any traces of dirt. And remember, anal bacteria are unhealthy for the vagina. No matter how clean you are, it pays to be careful. Once something has been in an ass, it shouldn't go in the pussy without a thorough cleaning with disinfectant soap.

Use gloves and condoms to keep the cooties off, and cleanup will be a snap.

Beyond the rectum lies the rest of the digestive system. Because it is not a cul-de-sac, as is the vagina, it is possible to lose things in the rectum. Anything that goes into the ass must have a means of retrieval. For toys, this means having a flared base that stays outside the pucker, or a string, a ring, a handle, or some other part that remains outside of the body.

One of the hallmarks of anal sex is that it requires more care and relaxation than other sex play. The tissues of the anus are not as resilient as those of the vagina, nor do they self-lubricate, so they can tear if treated roughly. Our anal sex mantra: "relaxation, communication,

A match made in heaven: the Pearl butt plug and a dollop of lube.

Sfera Duotone Balls

lubrication." Anal penetration can be entirely painless and utterly pleasurable. The keys to achieving that pleasure are going only as fast as your body is ready to go, and using lubricant to ease penetration.

ORGASM

Orgasm is the involuntary release of muscular tension that follows the buildup of arousal. The release of tension is usually characterized by a series of spasms a few seconds apart. How many and how intense the spasms are varies. Some people characterize it as fireworks, a small tremor, or a flood of well-being. Orgasm can be a localized sensation or a whole-body event. If you want stronger orgasms, one way to get them is to work those orgasmic muscles. There are many muscles in the pelvic area, the largest of which are the pubococcygeus, or PC, muscles, so we'll use that as shorthand to refer to all the muscles involved in orgasm. "Kegel" exercises tone the pelvic muscles (see "Feel the Burn, Baby" for suggested workout).

Because male orgasm typically requires a recovery period, that expectation is often erroneously projected onto women, too. The reality is that one orgasm doesn't knock most women out for the night; they can come back to excitement and orgasm after only a very short rest, or with no rest at all. Often,

Feel the Burn, Baby!

Make your orgasms stronger, your genital awareness more profound, and penetration feel better by developing your PC muscles. The PC muscles form a figure-eight shape, with one loop around the vagina and one around the anus. You can do these simple exercises at home or anywhere out in the world—no one can see what you're up to.

1. Locate your PC muscles by clenching the muscles you would use to stop the flow of urine.

2. Quick time: Do a series of quick clenches, 1-2-3-4-5. Now release.

3. Repeat, focusing the clench on your anal sphincters and muscles.

4. Slow it down—inhale slowly as you tighten up for one long clench. Release slowly upon exhaling.

5. Imagine sucking water up into your vagina or anus, then pushing it back out. Bear down.

6. Repeat this series of exercises 10 times a day, every day, and you'll soon tone up.

female orgasms pile up on one another like punks in a mosh pit, each new one adding to the intensity and excitement. The first orgasm may not be the strongest, so don't stop after just one! Subsequent orgasms can build up into an intense crescendo of coming.

What Men Have

As we've mentioned before, men and women have plenty of anatomical similarities. The structures of the clitoris are analogous to those of the penis, and the G-spot and the prostate are close cousins; as for assholes, everybody's got one. It's a bit easier to see what's going on genitally with men, as it's mostly hanging right out there, but it would be a mistake to assume that what you see is all of what you get. The prostate and the root of the penis both thrill to the stimulation of penetration. Everything we said about anal penetration for women applies to men, too. And, as with women, men can become multiorgasmic.

THE PENIS

We all know something about Mr. Happy, but here's a quick refresher on some of the male anatomical highlights. The penis jumps to attention when a man gets sexually excited. Blood surges in through arteries closer to the core of the penis, filling up waiting erectile tissue, while tension causes the vessels through which blood leaves the penis to squeeze shut. All that blood trapped in the penis causes an erection. The swollen penis becomes very sensitive to the touch, particularly around the head. On the underside of the ridge formed where the head connects to the shaft is the frenulum, an exquisitely sensitive spot. Extending from the frenulum down the shaft over the testicles and to the anus is a slightly raised ridge (the raphe), which is also quite sensitive. The penis extends into the pelvis to its root, which can be pleasurably stimulated through the perineum or with anal penetration.

All men are born with a foreskin, a loose sleeve of skin that covers the head of the penis. Removal of the foreskin (circumcision) is still common. It's traditional for Jews and Muslims and is a common practice for many in North America, regardless of religion. There is an active movement opposed to circumcision, as some people consider it an unnecessary modification that results in a loss of sensitivity.

Penis size varies more when flaccid than erect. Erect, most penises are about $5^{1}/2$ inches (14cm) long, so a man who is small when soft may turn out to be a "grower, not a show-er"; that is, when erect, his penis might be considerably larger than his flaccid size appears to indicate. Men get cast in porn movies based on their large penis size and ability to keep a hard-on, so if dirty movies are your standard of comparison, it's easy to feel inadequate. An average man is no more likely to have Jeff Stryker's dick than Brad Pitt's jawline. Remember the adage about it being "the motion of the ocean, not the size of the ship" that makes for a good voyage, so if your dick is not as large as you would like, let it be motivation to get

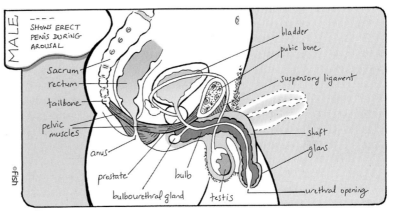

good at other aspects of sex. Men can also use toys and hands as a way to satisfy a partner who wants to be filled up.

It's also possible to have a penis that is uncomfortably large for your partner. A hand wrapped around the base can prevent it from going in too deeply, and lots of buildup with hands and toys can make it easier to accommodate girth. And don't forget the lube!

TESTICLES

Below the penis hang the testicles. Encased softly in their scrotal sac, these two balls are the source of sperm. Although testicles are incredibly sensitive to excessive pressure, many men enjoy light caresses, licking, or gentle tugging on their balls. Testicles vary a lot in size, not only between individuals but also in individuals, depending on arousal, temperature, and psychological state. It's common for men to have two differently sized testicles as well.

FAQ

Am I normal?

We get asked this question a lot, sometimes about body parts ("My clit is two inches long, is that normal?"), sometimes behaviors ("I prefer anal sex to vaginal sex, is that normal?"). Whatever your thing is, you're probably not the only one, but you may be one of a few. A more useful question is "Is this hurting anyone?" If the answer is no, then it's okay, no matter how common or not. The pressure to be "normal" is a real buzzkill for sexual happiness, which has so much to do with letting go.

ANUS AND PROSTATE

Men enjoy anal stimulation for all the same reasons women do, and then some. Through the anus both the prostate (sometimes known as the male G-spot) and the root of the penis can be stimulated. The prostate, a donut-shaped gland wrapped around the urethra, is pressure-sensitive. It can be stimulated through the front wall of the rectum. Gay men are often more familiar with their prostates, but every man has one. There is no good reason to believe that anal penetration isn't for straight boys, too. For some men, prostate play sends them out of this world; for others it is a pleasant addition to their sexual repertoire.

ORGASM

As a man approaches orgasm, his testicles pull up close to his body, and sperm leaves the testicles through a little tube called the *vas deferens*. As sperm passes the prostate gland on the way to the urethra and from there on to the great outside world, seminal fluid is added to the mix. The now full urethra puts pressure on the prostate, which sends a message to the spinal nerves. The message says, "I'm going to come!" Up until that message gets sent, a man can redirect his thoughts, change his breathing, or reduce stimulation to postpone orgasm and maintain his erection.

The Prostaterator

Toys in Babeland is run by women, so consequently gay men are our rarest customers. "What do we need with a bunch of vibrators?" they seem to be thinking. One day, a curious gay couple came in and wanted to know about everything. We showed them our best-selling Magic Wand vibrator and the G-spotter attachment that goes with it. Dubbing the attachment the "prostaterator," they made the purchase. Happily, one of them came back a few days later to report. "It was unbelievable," he said, "I hit the ceiling—it was like I was 18 again!" We tell this story as encouragement to all the guys out there who are shy about anal sex. Try it—it feels good!

(Men who choose to can learn to separate ejaculation from orgasm.) Once this communication has occurred, ejaculation is inevitable. As with women, men's orgasms vary in intensity and duration—it may be a localized sensation of excitement and release, or a mind-blowing climax. Physiologically, nerves fire, muscles contract, semen spurts out, and that's the end of the line for that erection. After ejaculation, most men take a while to recuperate (this is called the refractory period) before they can get another hard-on. For some men, however, especially teenagers, the refractory period can be quite brief; but as men mature, it usually takes longer. If a man can prevent himself from ejaculating, he will keep his erection. Men who want to stay hard longer usually do it two ways, either by learning to postpone orgasm or by learning to separate orgasm from ejaculation. No matter which approach they take to prolong their erections, the result is more of a total-body arousal. Some men get into this for their own satisfaction, while others are motivated by a desire to keep up with their partners. Men learn to be multiorgasmic through ejaculatory control (see below), or they can keep up with multiorgasmic partners using their hands, mouths, or sex toys.

That's a Wrap

Knowing all the details of sexual anatomy won't by itself make you a fabulous sex freak. What it can do is give you an idea of why some types of touch might feel good, so you'll think to give them a try. Although we all have the same basic anatomy, people vary a lot in what turns them on, for no reason other than personal preference. So if you've got a technique that is the total bomb for yourself or a lover, when you try it out on a different partner it might be a flop. If something tried and true doesn't go over well, knowing about bodies can help you come up with plan B. The elements you need to mix with knowledge and technique are sexual expressiveness and sensitivity: more about those in the next chapter.

Come Again?
The Multiorgasmic Male

There are two common techniques men use to become multiorgasmic. The first is learning to back off on the level of excitement just before the moment of "ejaculatory inevitability." This requires practice, usually starting with masturbation. After developing some skill, it's time to try it with a partner. The second method comes from Taoist traditions, and involves pressure points. A very shorthand version is to press firmly on your perineum just before orgasm and ejaculation. The pressure will prevent you from ejaculating. Without ejaculation, your cock will stay hard for more play. See Chapter Six, The Men's Room, for more.

Tower of power: the classic Slimline vibrator.

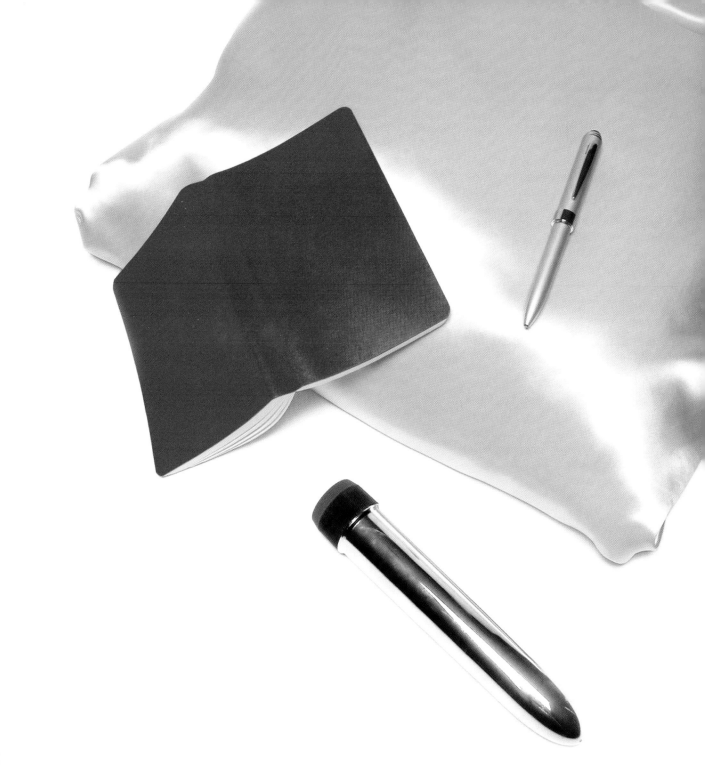

CHAPTER 2

sex on the brain

One year, at the Michigan Womyn's Music Festival, the Toys in Babeland crew was vending our wares, hooking women up with vibrators, dildos, safe sex gear, and the like. Into our booth walked a seventy-something-year-old woman with two much younger women. The younger women were her granddaughters, cousins to each other, as similar as bookends.

If those girls could have been anywhere else, they would have been. They were big-boned, tall, and strong-looking, but they carried

sexual expression & communication

themselves as if they were ashamed to take up so much space. Only their obedience to their grandmother could have brought them to a festival like Michigan, or to a store like Toys in Babeland. Neither of them said a word as their eyes took in the toys.

We greeted them, then let them have their privacy as they looked around. After a few minutes we asked them whether they

Dear Diary...Start an intimate journal; let the Vibrapen and the Silver Slimline inspire you.

needed any help. The girls looked startled and embarrassed, as though we had walked into their personal fantasies. The older woman, Alice, introduced herself and pulled up a seat, declaring, "I want to buy my granddaughters vibrators."

After a few more minutes the girls picked matching Freshman vibes, Alice paid, and as we put their toys in a bag she confided, "I just want them to know that their sexuality belongs to them. I hope their mothers don't get mad."

If only we all had a grandmother like Alice, poised to swoop in and counteract the negative messages we get about sexuality! As most of us don't, we have to forge our own path to accepting and loving our sexuality. Fortunately, with more and more helpful books, videos, and sex toys on the market every day, it's easier than ever to be your own fairy godmother.

Getting comfortable with our sexuality isn't easy. Most of us don't start out feeling entitled to sexual pleasure. As we struggle to acknowledge our desires and get them met, we come to discover over time that our sexuality is ours to explore and to express, and that it can be one of the greatest sources of energy and creativity in our lives. At Toys in Babeland, we see people at every stage of this process.

Your Erotic Map

There's more to great sex than anatomy. Knowing how the body works and where the important parts are helps, but desire and eroticism are the biggest factors. Everyone's got an erotic map, their own personal landscape of turn-ons and desires. Not only is each person's set of erotic hot buttons unique, but they may vary from day to day. Give yourself permission to develop your capacity for pleasure and to get to know yourself sexually. Sometimes slow, sensuous lovemaking is the ticket; other times you might yearn for an element of power. Maybe you require the sight or touch of feet to get turned on. Great sex means getting in touch with the spark of eroticism inside of you and giving it the fuel to keep burning bright.

Bubble Wand

Our reliance on visual cues means that looks are often considered central to desire. Busty blonde bombshells and tall, dark, handsome hunks are the standards mainstream culture promotes as ideals of desirability. Fortunately for us regular folks, you don't have to have movie star looks to enjoy a deeply satisfying sex life. Great sex is for everybody. Knowing that you're sexy, having a clue about what turns you on, and being able to communicate with a lover are far more vital than appearances.

You can learn how to have great sex just as you learned how to ride a bike. The myth that lovers should just fall into each other's beds and effortlessly have satisfying, connected, orgasmic sex fosters unrealistic expectations. You can learn skills and tricks to try with lovers that will enhance sex for both of you. As you discover more about what you like, you can tell your lovers about it, and the sex will get even better. Speaking up about what you want increases the chances that you'll get it, but it involves breaking the silence with which lovers protect themselves from hurt feelings or conflict. Many of us find ourselves tongue-tied when asked what we like in bed. "Everything you're doing is wonderful," we reply, thus preventing our lovers from doing more of that thing we *really* like. Speaking up comes from sexual self-confidence—a confidence that can be nurtured. Nurture it with masturbation, by developing your fantasy life, and by exploring (even if only in fantasy) different sexual possibilities.

Incremental delights: Blue Beads.

"Jilling" Off

Terms for female masturbation are few and far between. We like jilling off, pet your bunny, polish your pearl, and whip your cream. If you have a term you like to use, e-mail it to us—we want to expand the lexicon: rachel@babeland.com, claire@babeland.com.

Dialing O on the Pink Telephone

Betty Dodson calls masturbation "a love affair with ourselves that lasts a lifetime." Let that statement motivate you to spend more time on self-love. It's easy to treat masturbation as just servicing yourself, somewhere between flossing your teeth and making a sandwich on the scale of self-maintenance. While quick orgasms can be good mood elevators, if you put more into it, you'll get more out of it.

Both women and men can benefit from putting more energy into masturbation. Men who learned to masturbate in stolen moments often unintentionally train themselves to come quickly. Learning ejaculatory control always starts with masturbation, during which guys learn to slow down and enjoy more of a whole-body experience. Women are just as apt to get into the habit of getting off quickly. Slow down and spend some time with yourself, and you'll reap the rewards of a more satisfying sex life.

You can learn skills and tricks to try with lovers that will enhance sex for both of you.

Make a masturbation date with yourself. Set the scene for a sexy interlude: play music, light candles, or burn incense. Prepare your body as well. Take a shower or bath, slather yourself with lotion, or anoint yourself with scent. Dress up in a way that feels sexy to you. Sensuous fabrics promote sexy feelings.

How do I have an orgasm if I've never had one before?

Many of our women customers have never had an orgasm, or else aren't sure whether they have or not. Sometimes they haven't had the right stimulation; other times they're hobbled by sexual shame; most of the time it's a bit of both. But there is no reason why you shouldn't have all the orgasms you want. We suggest you start by spending good quality time masturbating: arouse yourself by using your hand and a vibrator on your clit, and by exploring your pussy with fingers and dildos—anything that helps you connect your feelings of desire with your body's sensations.

Beginners—all you need is some lube and your nimble fingers to start your exploration. Start by caressing yourself as you would a lover. Draw your energy and attention to your genitals by running your hands up your thighs and over your belly and your ass. As the heat builds, touch your pussy. If you are wet, pull some of the wetness from your vagina up and around your clit. Rub along the inside of your inner lips and over the hood of your clit; if direct contact with your clit feels good, go ahead and touch it. Squeeze some lube onto your fingers if you aren't wet, and spread it all around your pussy. Slickness is a turn on, so let the lube flow! Find a stroking rhythm that feels good and stick to it. Take your time and see where the rhythm takes you. Usually, once you have found the right motions, repetitive, rhythmic stroking will do the trick.

Those who have found that manual stimulation doesn't take you all the way to orgasm, apply vibration! The extra *oomph* from a vibrator might be just the ticket to take you on a fantastic trip! (Check out Chapter 3: What's the Buzz, for all you need to know about a woman's best friend.)

Maybe wearing a cowboy hat or fancy nail polish puts you in the mood. Whatever it is, go ahead. Do whatever helps you to feel good about yourself. Some people find that dancing helps them sink deeper into their bodies. Put on music you can groove to, and feel the rhythm. Alone in your space, let yourself move however you like. It may not look like the dancing you'd do at a nightclub, but that's okay. This is a time for permissiveness and going with the flow. If you like to look in mirrors, take a look. Dance with yourself. Move your consciousness down into your ass and genitals and get your pelvis rocking. Smile at that hottie in the mirror and give her or him a wink.

Feel yourself all over. You may be able to get off from some quick genital touch, but the more energy you put into getting aroused, the bigger and better your orgasm is going to be. So, get into it. Run your hands over your body, squeezing the muscles and stroking the soft places. Be sure to touch your nipples!

Some people like to focus on their bodily sensations as they masturbate. Others prefer to occupy their minds with fantasy. If you haven't experimented, try both. Even experienced masturbators can be pleasantly surprised when they do something different. Try new strokes and pressures just for the heck of it—you may stumble across a whole new way to get yourself off. The same goes for positions. Try it on all fours for a change.

As you touch yourself, first just move your hands, then begin to move the rest of your body, too. Pump your hips and squeeze your pelvic muscles. Clenching and releasing those muscles helps to build energy in the area. If it feels good, moan. Talking dirty to yourself pours fuel on the fire. If you don't know what to say, try saying out loud what is happening or what you're feeling: "I'm fucking myself, yeah, that's it, I'm fucking myself, it feels so good, I'm pushing my hips into it, yeah, that's right, I'm pushing and I'm fucking and pushing and fucking," and so on. It doesn't have to be poetry. Everything you do to express yourself— making noise, grinding, clenching, and touching— works toward making a deeper erotic connection.

While some people have no problem thinking up elaborate fantasies, others come up dry. But there are no rules to fantasy. Erotic stories can be memories, and can involve people you know, as well as strangers, celebrities, aliens, or animals. They might be narratives or only images. Sometimes one image over and over again, as in remembering the particular curve of someone's skin, is all it takes. Normally we think in a somewhat linear way, but masturbatory mental images can be endlessly repetitive without ever getting dull. If you can't come up with sexy fantasies or memories, seek erotic images from outside to turn your crank.

Cute and yellow and chubby: the Duckie Vibe.

FUEL FOR THE FIRE

Pornography and erotica come in all sorts of media: books, magazines, audio and video recordings, and websites. Whenever there's an advance in technology, the new gizmo is often used for sex. Blue movies were among the first motion pictures, and the biggest financial successes of the early Web days were the porn sites. Sexual taste varies so much that it's a safe bet there is something out there to attract or repulse anyone. So cast a broad net but don't be surprised if you haul in a few things you'll want to throw back. Try to keep your preconceived ideas of what you like in check; you may be surprised.

An erection (and that includes an erect clit) sometimes tells a truth that surprises the mind. And what appeals in fantasy may have little or no correlation to what you'd enjoy actually doing. If you're experimenting with pornography for the first time, head down to the video store and get a range of titles. Few porn films are worth watching from beginning to end—it'll be more fun if you have a stack of flicks to go through and use a heavy thumb on the fast-forward. Get at least one high-production value, big-budget Hollywood porn confection (maybe something by Michael Ninn or Brad Armstrong, porn auteurs known for good-looking product). And get something raunchy, a wall-to-wall sex thing that

> An erection (and that includes an erect clit) sometimes tells a truth that surprises the mind.

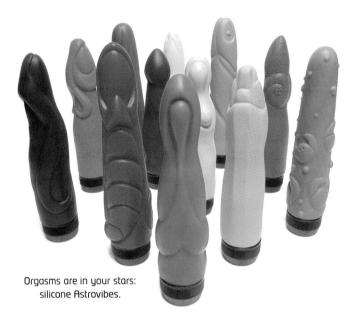

Orgasms are in your stars: silicone Astrovibes.

has more fuck energy than finesse. If you find porn degrading to women, look for work by female directors—Candida Royalle has a series with more than the usual emphasis on plot, character, and authentic portrayals of female pleasure. For true-to-life lesbian action, *How to Fuck in High Heels* is a good bet. Gay porn is a universe unto itself, one populated by incredibly good-looking guys. Falcon Studios produces hot stuff, but in this as in all cases, look at the box cover stills for actors or settings that pique your interest. Some people like to jack or "jill" off while watching, others save up the images to replay in their head later.

One-handed reading also offers a lot of possibilities. Regular "skin rags" offer airbrushed stills of young babes and studs, as well as some raunchy writing. *Penthouse Forum* has short fantasy vignettes masquerading as true stories. Other people's fantasies are fun, either as masturbation material or just for the "people are strange" factor. Nancy Friday has a series of collections of fantasies along with some analyses about why certain fantasies are so popular (those involving dogs, for example). If you are looking for more literary smut, you can find it in a wealth of collections, including these popular titles: *Best American Erotica*, *Best Gay Erotica*, *Best Lesbian Erotica*, and *Best Transgender Erotica*. Another route would be to revisit those early twentieth-century highbrow-smut writers, Anais Nin and Henry Miller.

There is a law in physics that states, "A body in motion tends to stay in motion." A similar principle applies to eroticism. As you read more sexy stories, watch more sexy movies, and spend more time making eyes at yourself in the bedroom mirror, your general state of erotic charge increases. So does your self-knowledge. After watching one of Ernest Greene's SM videos, an SM novice will know better whether that is the type of thing to float her boat. For people who haven't engaged in a lot of sexual experimentation, this kind of investigation can lead to an erotic blossoming. Feeling more in touch with that electric current in ourselves makes us feel more alive—and often more joyously connected to the world around us.

Talking to Your Lover

All this self-exploration has benefits for partner sex, too. As you become more sexually alive, comfortable with your body, and used to experimenting, it gets easier to take risks with a partner. It's a risk to ask for what you want. You could be rejected ("You want me to do what?!"), which would be disappointing, or you could hurt your lover's feelings. But the upside potential is outstanding. Not only can you get what you want (and why not have your toes sucked if you like it so much?) but you're also creating a climate of adventure and acceptance with your lover. Sex is playtime for adults, and just like kids, we don't want to play the same game day after day, year after year.

Even saying something as simple as "that feels good" builds communication with your lover. If you're shy, start with little bits of positive feedback, then as you develop your sexual voice, it will become

Ultraskin

Mr. Big

easier to be more specific, and to let your partner know what's not working in a lighthearted way. The more you talk, the less laden any given statement is. Many women are sexually shy because we don't want to rock the boat, or because we want to be "good girls." Forget all that! Sexual shyness just leaves us wishing and wondering.

Sharing fantasies is a great way to develop an exciting sex life. Fantasies are among our most private thoughts, and it can feel vulnerable to share, but that willingness to be vulnerable deepens an intimate connection. And maybe you can use your fantasies as raw material for real-life play. One of our friends had a long-cherished fantasy involving a secretary with a short skirt and an executive with a big desk and a big cock. Our poor feminist friend wanted to be the executive and felt ashamed of that reprobate idea. Imagine the delight when one day our friend's lover revealed that she had the exact same fantasy, but saw herself as the secretary. What joy! They play-acted their parts with a shared understanding that it was just make-believe and didn't represent their real beliefs about sex roles. Both parties retained their feminist credentials in each other's eyes.

Acting out fantasies can be as elaborate or as simple as the lovers desire. Just talking without any props is fun. Call the bed a desk and it's a desk, if you both agree. Costuming adds more kick to the game. Dress the executive in a three-piece suit and give the secretary a clipboard, and it may get even hotter.

Even if your fantasies don't dovetail as nicely as our friends' did, sharing them is still a way to find common interests that you might not have known about. If you are willing to indulge your sweetie in some quirks and kinks, chances are that he or she will stretch to meet you, too, and your sex life will become a lot more varied and interesting.

FAQ

How can I get my lover to tell me what he or she likes?

Sometimes a question as simple as "What do you want?" can be overwhelming. If your sweetie clams up, try giving a choice, "Do you prefer this ... or this?" to get an answer. Give positive feedback—and be patient. Not everyone loves sex talk, and some people get so into their own body sensations that they seem to lose their words. Attend to physical signs of pleasure, such as rapid breathing, flushing, and muscle tension.

SMUTTY MOUTHS AND DRESSING UP

Talking dirty is simply sexual communication turned to high. Instead of just sharing information and offering encouragement, dirty talk turns up the temperature by being sexy in and of itself. It can take a while to get used to the four-letter words that convey in the most graphic terms what you want. For some folks "penis" and "vagina" are as raunchy as they want to go. But most agree that "dick" and "cock" are more sexually powerful than "penis," just as there are juicier words for "vagina." A lot of graphic sex words like "cunt" and "pussy" have been used as slurs, so they take a little work to get comfortable with. Just as "queer" has been reclaimed by the gay community as a positive descriptive word, women are reclaiming "cunt." Eve Ensler, in her hit show "The Vagina Monologues," exhorts the women in the audience to say "cunt" as loudly and as forcefully as they can. Try it! Say it out loud right now: "Cunt, cunt, cunt."

Cunt is the first word we get back, and pussy is on the second boat from the land of the forbidden to the shores of the pleasurable. We have seen lots of stickers out there that say "pussy power," and there is even a pro-sex, feminist book titled *Cunt: A Declaration of Independence*, by Inga Muscio. Those terms are clearly on the way up. For those who bridle at such graphic expressions, the Hindi term *yoni* is a more goddess-inflected choice. It's hard to communicate without

descriptive words, so try these out and see whether they work for you. Or make up your own special words.

Dirty talk doesn't have to be sailor's talk, unless you want it to be. The idea is to incorporate aural stimulation into the sex. Some people like to

Hooking Up

If you've got specific characteristics you want in a lover—either physical attributes or sexual preferences—it can be both a blessing and a curse. It shrinks the pool of potential playmates, but if you know what you want up front you're more likely to get it. Gay men lead the way in this. Their personal ads aren't composed of people looking for "HWP, financially stable, enjoys going out, seeks same"-type notices. They give a good physical description and then move on to the stuff they enjoy: "Loves giving oral," "Seeks hairy men of all ages and races," "Must call me Daddy," and so on.

Any blind date is a risk, but these kinds of specifics increase the chances that they'll be sexually compatible with their potential partners. If what you're looking for is a date or an affair, try a personal ad—and be as precise as you can about what you want.

Bondage Tape

Novelty is a great source of sexual excitement, which is one reason new relationships are often lost-weekend sex-fests, while long-term relationships are sometimes more tepid. To keep the flame burning bright, pay attention to the sexual relationship. In our experience, the couples who seem to be most joyously involved with each other sexually look at turning each other on as a shared adventure. Often there is a lightness and laughter to their demeanor in the store, even when they are intensely interested in something. It's not a case of "this vibrator better fix what's wrong in our relationship." That's a lot of pressure for one little appliance. A sex toy can enhance sex, but it cannot be a life preserver for a relationship that's going down for the third time.

describe what is happening: "My hands are grabbing your ass." Others like to promise upcoming delights: "... then I'm going to slide my finger up your ass." While still others like to describe what could be happening: "We're in the middle of the desert, naked in the blazing sun, and we're covered in oil, stroking each other's asses." They're all ways to express yourself and create a more intense sexual experience.

Dressing up is sexy, too. One of the best bars in San Francisco is the Eagle. The Eagle is a gay men's leather bar, and the men there create a very sexy vibe. They dress up for the occasion, usually in blue jeans, big black boots, tight T-shirts, and buzz cuts. No silk shirts or expensive designer suits for them. Their outfits express the ways in which they feel sexy. For you it might be strappy sandals or tailored suits. Dressing up exhibits your body for your own pleasure. But you can also dress up to turn your partner on. Some people like to create elaborate costume dramas while acting out their fantasies. But don't wear clothes that make you feel uncomfortable in any way. That will throw a wet blanket on your sexual fire.

The keys to long-term sexual happiness are self-knowledge, expressiveness, vulnerability, sharing, and novelty. Self-knowledge is all about exploring your own fantasies and knowing what turns you on, and expressiveness is telling your partner. For sex to remain exciting it's got to be about more than just physically going through the motions. It requires being fully present with the other person, being able to look them in the eyes while doing it. If you're harboring secrets or sexual resentment it's hard to meet your lover's eyes. That's where the vulnerability comes in. Exposing yourself makes you vulnerable to rejection but open to connection, too. Put yourself out there to fully connect with your partner. Whether or not they meet you is up to them, but in a long-term relationship, unless both people are willing to expose their desire for connection, the sex will probably become flat and boring.

Sharing the sexual adventure with your partner is a bit like sharing an adventure such as mountain climbing or river rafting. It's exciting and scary. Telling your partner your thoughts and fantasies is a risk. There's a chance your partner might not meet you with excitement about whatever you've revealed. The more confident you are in yourself (and this is where knowing that you can give yourself orgasms, feel sexy, and enjoy life without your partner helps a lot), the easier it is to expose yourself. It's a bit of a paradox. The more you don't *need* your partner, the more able you will be to open up to him or her. That's another reason sex with a new lover is hot. You don't really need someone you've been with for two weeks, so it's easy to expose a lot.

As a relationship progresses and the involvement deepens, the stakes become higher. As rejection becomes a less tolerable outcome, it's tempting to stop taking risks. But great sexual highs come from ecstatic sexual connection, and the connection comes from exposing yourself. Relationships will thrive sexually if the partners risk emotional connection. Experimenting with sexual tricks and toys can be part of that. But you have to be sharing the adventure first. That's why no vibrator alone can ever save your relationship.

Lifelong Sex

Great sex is about following the spark of desire. If it was merely about learning techniques of masturbation or giving pleasure to a partner, we could all take a course, receive our certification, and that'd be the end of it. But erotic spark is a moving object. What generates the heat when you're 19 is probably different from when you are 40. And what generates heat at 7:30 Saturday night might not be sexy at 10:30 Sunday morning. It's that fresh regeneration of excitement that makes sex such an "in your body" experience. Hot sex requires you to be present, to follow the spark of your own desire, to communicate that with your partners, and to return again and again to the willingness and to the surprise of what is revealed.

Try This

As you find out about your own sexuality, write it down! Keeping a sex diary can help build your awareness of your sexuality as it develops and changes. Your sexuality is like your dream life—it can be hard to remember exactly what happens during such intense experiences. As the entries accumulate, you may be surprised by what you find when reading back through your book. In the privacy of your diary, you can be as explicit and candid as you want to be. It's for no one's eyes but your own.

Silicone Stretch
Cock Rings

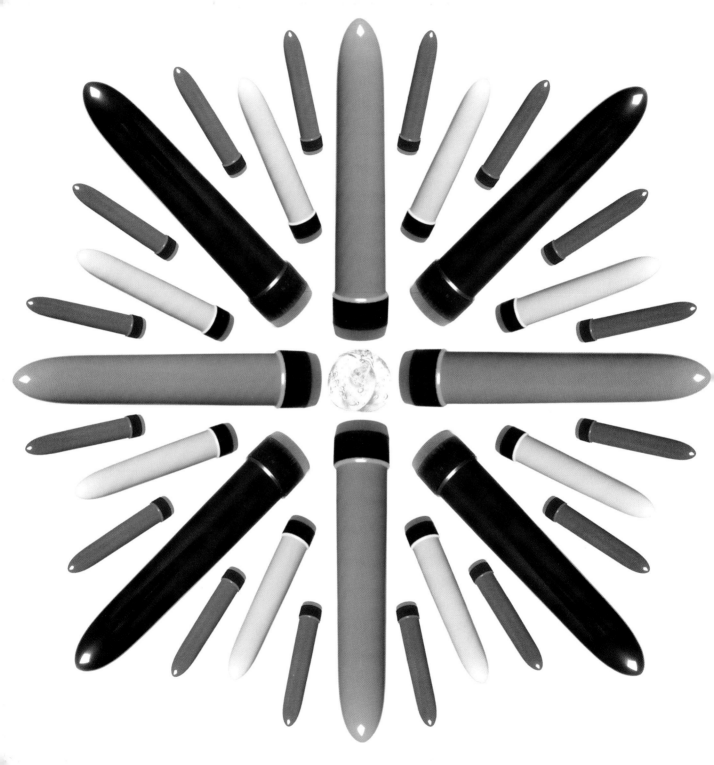

CHAPTER 3
what's the buzz?

all about vibrators

"PUTTING MORE WOMEN INTO ORBIT IN A WEEK THAN NASA HAS IN A LIFETIME," shouted our advertisement for the Pocket Rocket, a petite but powerful vibrator. Little did we know how many women longed to leave Earth's gravity! We'd witnessed various vibrators come in and out of vogue, but we were unprepared for the stampede that followed the introduction of the Pocket Rocket. Maybe people were looking for permission to add a vibrator to their sex lives; maybe it was the perky, spark plug—like profile of the toy. Whatever the reason, during the winter holidays, 1999, New York City caught Pocket Rocket fever, and our store looked like San Francisco at the height of the Gold Rush.

The customers, mostly men, crowded into the store. Wall Street guys in expensive suits, construction workers on their lunch break, city employees in uniform—men of every description found their

Visions of Vibrators... the classic Slimline delivers the vibes— and comes in a rainbow of colors.

way to Babeland to pick up what seemed to be the season's most coveted sex toy. Many claimed their girlfriends told them not to come home without one. Several men bought five or six of them. After a week or two of this kind of response, our customers didn't even have to speak. Shy guys sidled up to the counter and passed us the crumpled ad they had torn out of the newspaper. We saw them coming and just handed over the vibrator. No grown woman's stocking was properly stuffed without the Pocket Rocket that year.

Shortly after the turn of the millennium, New York seemed to breathe a collective, post-orgasmic sigh of relief. Toys in Babeland Sex Educators joked that all those holiday Pocket Rockets must have alleviated New York's neuroses and anxieties as no psychoanalyst could. Was it our imagination, or was everyone in New York nicer to one another after that gift-buying season?

Finally, the clitoris is out of the closet, and vibrators are everywhere!

The Clit Comes Out of the Closet

Most women absolutely require direct clitoral stimulation to achieve orgasm—and the powerful, consistent stimulation of a vibrator delivers like nothing else can. The extra oomph on the clitoris that a vibrator provides is just what many women need to come—whether alone or with a partner. Vibrators have helped many pre-orgasmic women to reach that longed-for first orgasm, and have brought reliable satisfaction to many others. Today, more women than ever are introducing vibes into partner sex. Using a vibrator with her partner means a woman can enjoy all that powerful, sexy, turned-on energy she and her partner are generating, then add the extra push of vibration—and come. What a relief!

Luckily, the sex-toy revolution has made it to the mainstream. Over the last decade, we have watched happily as vibrators have achieved a remarkable measure of acceptability in popular culture. A charmingly daring Ikea ad features a toddler who has found Mommy's vibrator—he sits, chortling with glee as this new toy rattles across the floor. The slogan (acknowledging that sex toys are common enough to qualify as clutter) is "Tidy up!" And in an episode of HBO's *Sex in the City*,

Blast off with the Pocket Rocket!

one of the characters steps out of the dating pool to spend an entire weekend alone with her twirling, fluttering Rabbit Habit sex toy.

Popular men's magazines now proclaim that a man who goes on a date but neglects to bring a pocket-size vibrator may be somewhat less than completely prepared—*The Source* magazine published a sidebar featuring Ice-T recommending that men carry a Pocket Rocket every time they go nightclubbing. High-circulation women's magazines such as *Glamour* and *Essence* feature product reviews of vibrators alongside the latest in fashions and home furnishings.

Finally, the clitoris is out of the closet, and vibrators are everywhere!

A Short History of Vibrators

Vibrators got their start during the industrial revolution as medical devices; they were used to treat "hysteria" in women. At the time, hysteria was a catchall diagnosis that included a wide array of women's medical complaints, from simple irritability to debilitating physical weakness. These symptoms were considered by many medical experts to be the result of a prolonged lack of sexual gratification. Despite a widespread belief that unfulfilled sexual yearning could cause disease, proper nineteenth-century society women were supposed to disdain sex; so it is little wonder that many of them had not learned to reach orgasm, either by masturbating or having sex with their husbands. Acceptable sexual relations existed exclusively within marriage, were performed solely for purposes of procreation, and were limited to intercourse

Just what the doctor ordered: a vintage vibrator.

A homemaker's favorite appliance: the Bakelite Vibra-King.

to the point of male orgasm. Because sex for pleasure was frowned upon, all but the most traditional sex positions were taboo, and then, as now, the missionary position left most women wanting. A woman who did not get sexual satisfaction from intercourse alone was considered dysfunctional, which meant that orgasmically speaking, she was out of luck. Imagine the frustration!

It was clear to the doctors who treated their symptoms that these ladies were in dire need of medical attention. The form of that attention was quite often manual stimulation of the patient's genitals, performed by the doctor himself. (Why did the prescription never involve the husband paying attention to what might bring on the wife's orgasm in the marital bed? *Hmmm.*) As this treatment became commonplace, vibrators were developed as labor-saving devices. No more tedious hands-on stimulation of sexually dysfunctional women! Affluent women often enjoyed the convenience of physicians who made house calls. The ailing woman would respond to the doctor's ministrations with revitalizing paroxysms, and arise ready to face life again.

By the early part of the twentieth century, however, the vibrating cure had fallen from public favor. The first "blue movies," produced in the 1910s and '20s, often depicted a woman enjoying a sexual romp with a vibrator. That direct association with pleasure stripped vibrators of their medical camouflage. Once fallen from the "purity" of the medical world into the tawdry realm of pornography, vibrators were trapped in their association with sleaze until the 1960s, when feminist Sex Educators like Betty Dodson, Del Williams, and Joani Blank promoted them as valuable tools for pleasure.

Thanks to the sexual revolution, women today can finally feel entitled to a pleasure-filled sex life. The clitoris has been recovered from the trash can where Freud thoughtlessly tossed it a century ago, along with his now-debunked theory that vaginal orgasms are separate from and superior to clitoral orgasms. (So complete was the destruction of the clitoris' reputation that by the 1950s, some medical textbooks showed a blank spot where the clitoris should be!) The vibrator is an immensely helpful device for stimulating the clit and is finally achieving mainstream recognition—and it's about time! Vibrators have gone from being clinical instruments to titillating bachelorette party gifts, from naughty novelties to playful-yet-serious implements for sexual healing and liberation. We have watched and applauded the past decade of this burgeoning acceptance from our perch behind the counter at Toys in Babeland.

Today, women feel entitled to a pleasure-filled sex life.

Vibrators come in a jaw-dropping variety of styles and types. The main differences among them are their power source, what they are made of, and the kinds of stimulation they can provide.

Electric vibrators, or "plug-ins," are manufactured and marketed as muscle massagers, but in the context of a sex toy store, they stand out as the queens of quality and reliability. Battery-operated vibrators come from the sex toy industry, and are known for their endless variation rather than their staying power. Both kinds of vibrators have their merits and drawbacks; sex toy consumers might want to try one of each type to see which best suits their needs or ignites their fantasies. Remember, you don't have to be monogamous with your sex toys.

Remember, you don't have to be monogamous with your sex toys.

There are several materials to choose from. Jelly rubber, which has a pliable rubbery feel, and hard plastic or vinyl make up the majority of vibrators. Jelly is the softest, and most customers say it feels better for that reason. Cheap and easy to work with, it is the preferred material of most large sex toy manufacturers. As much as we love the feel of the jelly toys, however, the material is porous, so it's hard to keep clean. Children's toys made from jelly rubber have recently been banned in Europe; extended contact with skin may be unhealthy, so use a condom with jelly rubber toys.

Vinyl is softer than hard plastic and smoother than jelly. Vinyl toys should also be sheathed with a condom. Hard-plastic vibrators absorb less vibration than their softer counterparts, which means they send more of the sensations straight on to you. The drawback of hard-plastic toys (other than being hard) is that they are louder than the softer vibes. Jelly and vinyl muffle the sound.

The best material for vibrators, as for dildos, is silicone, because it's extremely easy to clean and has a wonderful, resilient feel. Unfortunately, few vibrator manufacturers have ventured into working with silicone because it's a much more expensive material. Still, there are several silicone vibrators on the market, our favorite of which is the Astrovibe, from a German company that makes a specially shaped vibrator for each sign of the horoscope.

Here's a closer look at the types of vibrators and the kinds of stimulation you might encounter in your search for the right rocket to send you to the stars.

Signs of spring: the Butterfly Vibe.

ELECTRIC VIBRATORS

Readily available in many drugstores and marketed as massagers intended to treat sore backs and shoulders, electric vibrators are the faithful friends found in many a woman's top drawer. Though they have all the visual charm of a kitchen appliance (even less since Philippe Starck started his line at Target), these vibrators are wonderfully successful at bringing women to orgasm through clitoral stimulation. Now a woman can have an orgasm at virtually any time she has an electric outlet and a few moments to spare. Unlike many sex toys that are marketed as "novelties," electric vibes are usually well made and will last for years. They come in three major varieties: wand-style vibes, rechargeable vibes, and coil vibes.

> **Now a woman can have an orgasm any time she has an electric outlet and a few moments to spare.**

Wand-style vibrators are the most powerful. The godmother of masturbation, Betty Dodson, supplies each of the attendees at her masturbation workshops with one as they come through the door. For women who have never had an orgasm, wand massagers are the best, because their powerful, insistent vibration is as close to a guarantee as the sex toy world can offer.

Rechargeable vibrators are versions of the wand that have built-in, rechargeable nickel-cadmium batteries. You plug them in to charge up, then detach the cord to allow for about half an hour of unencumbered, swinging-from-the-chandeliers fun.

Coil massagers are shaped like hand-held mixers and vibrate at a slightly higher pitch than the wands. The great advantage of coil vibes is that they are nearly silent—a nice feature for those who find buzzing intrusive or who worry about a household member detecting that telltale whirring.

Many of these styles are virtually unchanged since they were first marketed in the 1940s, and people occasionally send us old coil vibes they found in their grandma's attic. No matter which electric vibrator you choose, be prepared to develop a strong attachment to it. One Toys in Babeland Sex Educator buys her Wahl 7-in-1 a dozen roses every Valentine's Day.

The following vibrators have been elected to Toys in Babeland's Electric Vibrator Hall of Fame:

Rolls Royce of vibrators: the Hitachi Magic Wand.

Hitachi Magic Wand

Hail the supreme vibrator of vibrators. More than one female customer has come marching into the store, walked straight up to the Magic Wand, and stated, "I'll take one of these." These single-minded customers are there because after 12, 18, or even 20 years of dedicated service,

G-Whiz

their beloved Magic Wand has finally given out. The gorgeous colors and fancy actions of newer models cannot tempt these loyalists. The Hitachi Magic Wand is the One, and there can be no other. One lesbian couple bought two, one for each side of the bed. "What if we both have our period at the same time?" they pointed out to an inquiring friend. (The thudding buzz of the Magic Wand does wonders for menstrual cramps.) "And aside from that, she likes hers and I like mine, and it's just more convenient that way."

The Magic Wand is a solid, 12-inch (30cm) long appliance with a firm tennis-ball size head most popular for clit stimulation, though many guys also like to use it on their penises. The head is just soft enough to make it comfortable against the genitals, but owing to the intensity of the vibration, some people prefer to use it through their underwear, a blanket, or a pillow. Even through a pillow it delivers deep vibration. Several attachments are available for the Magic Wand to adapt the appliance for penetration. Our favorite is the "G-Whiz," a silicone cup-and-dildo attachment that fits snugly over the head of the wand. It's safe for vaginal or anal penetration, and sends all the throbbing vibration of the wand straight to the G-spot or the prostate.

Wahl 7-in-1 This versatile coil massager comes with seven textured heads designed for use on different massage points on the body. The rounded heads focus the vibration for excellent clitoral stimulation. Additional attachments for penetration are sold separately. The great virtues of the Wahl are its silent, dependable buzz and innocuous design. It tops our list of discreet, well-made vibes that can be trusted to get the job done.

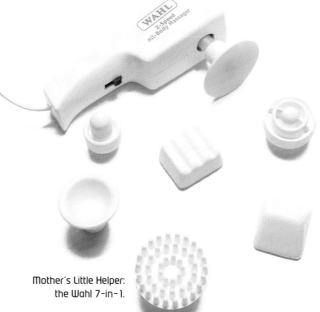

Mother's Little Helper:
the Wahl 7-in-1.

BATTERY-OPERATED VIBRATORS

The majority of battery-operated vibrators are designed and produced expressly for sex. The variety of shapes and styles is truly staggering. If necessity is the mother of invention, then sex is the very bedrock of human need. To make the selection a little simpler, we've divided the battery-operated vibes into two main categories: the dual-action vibes, which are *la crème de la crème* in the category; and what we like to call our "battery stalwarts," which include bullet vibes, mini massagers, G-spot stimulators, waterproof vibes, remote-control units, and "hands-free" vibes.

Dual-Action Dynamos

Dual-action vibes consist of two components: a twirling shaft for vaginal penetration and a clit stimulator. The two parts move independently, and each has its own control, so they can be adjusted for the particular preferences of the user. The clitoral attachment is usually shaped like a charming woodland creature or a goldfish. Made of soft molded vinyl, the attachment encases a vibrating egg, and its tongue, ears, or tail (depending on the model) is perfectly placed to flutter on the clitoris.

Japanese manufacturers make the best-quality battery-operated vibrators

Women's number 1
vibrating dream date:
the Rabbit Habit.

If It Looks Like a Toy...

The premium dual-action wonder-vibes from Japan feature heads in the shapes of geisha or samurai and animal-shaped clit ticklers, because in Japan it is reportedly illegal to manufacture a toy that resembles a penis. The origin of the law is in question—it is widely believed that the United States put it in place after World War II. While the head of the rotating shaft looks like the head of a penis in profile, upon close inspection it turns out to be a female head with a tiny face framed by a bob haircut, wearing a necklace of pearls. These quirks have not diminished the toys' popularity, however. An entire generation of women has come to eroticize bunnies and samurai faces on the strength of what these toys can do.

in the world. They cost more, but they do more and last longer than other battery-driven sex toys. It's tempting to say that you get what you pay for, but shoddy, cheaply made knockoffs can cost as much or more in typical sex toy stores—so beware of the fakes!

The Rabbit Habit is the cream of the dual-action crop. The toy's name is derived from the buzzing, purple rabbit whose ears form the clit-tickling centerpiece of the toy. In addition to the bunny and the twirling shaft, the Rabbit Habit comes with a unique feature: a generous belt of pearls set around the base of the shaft. These pearls tumble and cascade as the shaft rotates, offering stimulation around the opening of the vagina. The rotating shaft provides G-spot stimulation, and in the throes of passion—or of passionate masturbation—it can almost feel alive. One woman describes the fluttering ears as "almost like two tiny tongues stroking my clit." The only thing this Rabbit won't do is bring you chocolate eggs.

Battery Stalwarts

The rest of the battery-operated vibe realm contains a dizzying array of units, from pure novelty items to tried-and-true classics. Here we describe six different styles, and have elected one or two vibes as "best of breed" in each category to help you understand the differences.

A bullet-shaped vibrator consists of a vibrating plastic oval (the bullet) attached by a long wire cord to a battery pack. This is the throbbing heart of many vibrators in which the basic bullet is topped with a vinyl or cyber-skin covering. Hundreds of toys are made using this model. There are also dildos and accessories designed to work in conjunction with bullet-shaped vibrators. Because most bullets are cheaply made, buying a toy from which the vibrator can be removed saves money in the long run, particularly in the case of toys made from expensive silicone, which last much longer than the cheaply made bullet.

The Silver Bullet vibrator is a toy-chest workhorse. The shiny silver ovoid is perfectly shaped to fit into a variety of sheaths, harnesses, silicone dildos, or just to nestle into a pair of panties. Powered by two AA batteries, this little dynamo whirs with surprising intensity and often lasts for years. All for less money than some people spend on a day's worth of espresso drinks.

Heigh ho, Silver, away!
The Silver Bullet vibrator.

FAQ

Can I put my bullet vibrator inside myself?

Bullet-style vibrators are safe to use in the vagina but not in the anus. Bullets without a fancy vinyl covering are best for insertion. They are ideal for clitoral stimulation and suitable for vaginal insertion, but the wire connecting the battery pack to the vibrating piece is not meant to withstand pulling, so keep it out of your butt. The toy will last longer if you slip it in a condom before popping it in, and then remove it by pulling on the condom instead of the wire.

Honey Bears

The Honey Bear is a high-quality bullet vibe embedded in a soft, pink vinyl bear. The bear's arms arc over its head, reaching up to give the clitoris a vibrating hug. This is another example of the animal motif in Japanese vibrators, and has inspired the Honey Bear fans among our staff to invent the "Honey Bear Salute"—they throw their arms up into the same position as the bear's, proudly acknowleding their allegiance to this adorable, powerful toy.

Mini-massagers are junior versions of their plug-in siblings. Most are just as dependable, and just as bland-looking, but for scores of people, they fit the bill exactly.

The Pocket Rocket resembles a spark plug, and while that may not sound sexy, its innocuous look is what ushers it into thousands and thousands of bedrooms around the world every year. Purse-size, light, and streamlined, it appeals to many women who suspect they could benefit from using a vibrator but are new to the world of sex toys. They gravitate toward toys like the Pocket Rocket, which look less like the horse-size phalluses of popular imagination and more like a cigarette lighter or lipstick container. The Pocket Rocket is designed solely for clit stimulation.

The Pocket Rocket is also the best known of the neutral, non-sexual-looking vibrator camp. In fact, "Pocket Rocket" has become synonymous with "vibrator" in many people's minds. Since its surge in popularity, the sex toy industry has produced dozens of variations, including a waterproof version called the Waterdancer, and the I-Vibe, which comes in all the colors of the original iMac. There is even a Pocket Rocket–size vibe that's shaped like Hello Kitty, a popular Japanese cartoon character.

Also popular among the battery-operated vibrators are those specially curved to stimulate the G-spot. Until recently, most sex toy manufacturers were not known for their sensitivity to or understanding of female sexual anatomy. But G-spot vibrators take female sexual anatomy into account, with a curved "hook" that puts pressure right on the G-spot. The

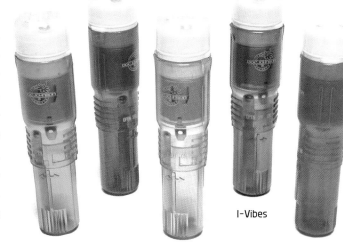

I-Vibes

better designs target vibration in the first third of the vagina, where nerve endings respond best to vibration. G-spot vibrators are made from soft or hard plastic or vinyl, and should have a firm curve. If they are too floppy the curve will straighten out when squeezed by vaginal muscles.

Among the legions of vibrators designed to hit the G-spot, one stands alone.

Nubby G The Nubby G has three advantages over the other models: its three-finger width, its just-right firmness, and its translucent good looks. The G-spot responds to firm pressure, and the Nubby G's pudginess allows for a wide area of massage-like pressure, while also providing a satisfyingly full feeling in the vagina. It's made of a clear, rubbery material that has just enough give so as not to poke uncomfortably, yet enough rigidity to prevent a collapse on the job. At least two Toys in Babeland Sex Educators have experienced ejaculation for the first time while using it. Among its biggest fans, it's known as the Nubby "Genius"!

The recent boom in waterproof vibe design acknowledges that the bath, shower, and hot tub can be sexy places, and waterproof vibrators have brought the thrill of orgasm to women who want to replace Rubber Ducky with more fun in the tub. On the practical side, the bathroom is recognized universally as a place where people have privacy. Few things are more private for most people than masturbation. Enter the waterproof vibrator. These toys add a new meaning to the phrase "singing in the shower"!

Waterproof vibes are also useful for those who ejaculate a lot and don't want to worry about keeping their toys dry when their minds are on other things.

Aqua Allstar The dark-blue jelly Allstar has a clit-stimulating branch that juts out from the larger shaft meant for vaginal insertion. It's about $1^1/2$ inches (a little less than 4cm) in diameter, a thick-ish size that lots of women like. The two branches make this a versatile vibe for clitoral, vaginal, or anal stimulation.

Cosmic Vibe

Try a curved vibe for special G-spot stimulation.

Aqua Allstar

Hawaiian Vibe This slim, hard-plastic vibe updates the classic obelisk-shaped vibe with a flowery pattern and an all-important water-proofing washer that protects the battery chamber. If Gidget goes surfing these days, this will most likely be in her beach bag.

Hawaiian
Vibe

Thanks to improvements in wireless technology, today's sexual adventurer can thrill a lover from across a crowded room. Small, remotely controlled vibrators are being built into panties or encased in butt plugs. Discreet switches activate these vibrators from distances of several yards away, much like a child's remote-controlled race car, but with much smaller components and purely adult results! Other advancements have allowed more and more powerful vibrators to come in smaller and more affordable packages. These tiny vibrators are built onto elastic harnesses to hold them perfectly in place, or are buried in the fingertips of gloves to make for a James Bond–style sex mitt.

FAQ

Can my vibrator give me an electrical shock?

We have never heard of a vibrator turning on its owner in this way. Obviously, you should keep electric vibes away from the bathtub. The only vibrator-related injury we have heard of is a burn caused by a Rabbit Pearl that heated up under a woman's belly after she rolled over on top of the still-buzzing toy to take a post-orgasmic nap. So, stay awake long enough to turn off your toy!

Fukuoku The hottest new vibrator sensation of recent years is the Fukuoku 9000. This small, candy-colored vibe packs powerful vibration into a small package that slips over the tip of a finger, like a vibrating thimble or a sexy decoder ring. It has a strong buzz, is fairly quiet, and doesn't take any effort to hold. This tiny vibe can be easily incorporated into partner sex. Wherever you use your fingers to caress your lover, the Fukuoku adds vibration to the mix.

A new generation of vibrators is designed to bathe the clitoris in vibration during penetration. The hallmarks of these vibes are their small size and hands-free operation. A flexible ring allows some models to be attached to a penis, dildo, or hand for clitoral stimula-

Thrills at your fingertips: five Fukuokus.

tion during penetration. Another popular design is the "vibro-panty" variation, which uses elastic straps to hold the toy against a woman's clit while she and her lover concentrate on other things.

Dolphin Ring Vibe This cute, pink sea creature is a bubble of soft, stretchy jelly over a miniature vibe. The stretchy ring makes it easy to wrap around practically anything you intend to put inside. On a flesh-and-blood penis, it does double duty as a cock ring and a vibe (see chapter 6). Once in place the little dolphin angles up perfectly to dive in for clitoral stimulation. A small battery pack can be tucked discreetly out of the way.

Micro Rocket For hands-free fun, this little silicone-covered vibe comes with thin, adjustable straps to hold the Rocket snug on the clitoris without obstructing the vagina. This toy seamlessly brings vibration into partner sex. It's also fun for the adventurous masturbator— that woman you see smiling inexplicably on the bus may have discovered the pleasures of the wearable vibe!

FAQ

How long will my vibrator last?

It depends on the quality of the vibrator you buy, the care you give it, and how frequently you use it. Vibrators produced by appliance companies, such as Hitachi or Wahl, are warranted by the manufacturer for one year but can last 20 years or more. High-quality Japanese-made toys can run for years as well, while cheaper Taiwanese or Chinese models may poop out in only a few months.

Common Concerns

One of the prickliest challenges and greatest rewards of selling sex toys is helping customers get past the anxieties that sex toys can bring up. A large proportion of our customers are first-time toy buyers, and they share many apprehensions about using vibrators to reach orgasm. With these customers we do some of our most satisfying work, allaying their fears and giving them permission to reach for the sexual satisfaction that some of them have never had.

The fact is, vibrators help women come, and coming is one of life's great pleasures. We assure our customers that literally millions of women rely on vibrators to reach orgasm at least some of the time. And even if a woman hasn't

> The fact is, vibrators help women come, and coming is one of life's great pleasures.

Heavy Metal Vibe

How to Choose a Vibrator: A Checklist

The truly amazing variety of vibrator styles, sizes, and materials can be both inspiring and a little daunting. Finding the perfect vibe may require some self-loving homework. Answering these few simple questions can help cut through the information overload and prevent buyer's remorse.

● WHAT DO YOU WANT TO USE IT FOR?

Do you want to use it on your clitoris? Do you want to put it in your vagina or anus? Because just about anything that vibrates feels good on or around the clitoris, phallic-shaped vibrators suitable for penetration can also be used outside the vagina if the vibration is strong at the tip. Do you want both the full feeling of penetration and that all-important clitoral buzz? Dual-action vibes mean never having to choose one feeling at the expense of the other. Electric

Sunflower Vibe

vibrators are the most powerful, so if you have a more difficult time orgasming, you may want to try one of those first.

If you intend to use a toy for anal insertion, make sure it has a flared base so that it doesn't slip all the way in. While there are vibrating toys made especially for anal use, most are not, so it's best to get one specifically designed for anal play, if that's what you fancy.

● HOW STRONG DO YOU WANT YOUR VIBRATION TO BE?

If you've never used a vibrator before, this is tough question to answer with certainty, so prepare to experiment! If you masturbate with a firm rub on the clit rather than a light touch, you're more likely to appreciate a strong vibration. Plug-in models vibrate the most powerfully, while jelly-rubber vibes that use only one AA battery vibrate the least intensely. Pick a toy with a variable speed control so you can play around until you discover just what amount of vibration starts your motor. After some initial investigation, you'll be ready to home in on your vibrating dream date.

● HOW MUCH DO YOU WANT TO SPEND?

Though the Silver Bullet is the least expensive vibrator we sell, it's quite strong and very good-looking. Some people like to start with a few of the cheaper ones and test them out. But if the deluxe, spinning, fluttering dual-action Japanese vibrator is within your budget, and you have a sense that it will float your boat, by all means skip the preliminaries and go for it.

Superbe

Discreet purse-size toys like the Pocket Rocket hold a lot of appeal for those on the go. But if your vibrator is never going far beyond your bedside drawer, size may not be a concern. Plug-ins are not portable but offer the most bang for the buck by outlasting their battery-powered cousins by years. If you plan to use the vibe for penetration, the girth of the toy may be just as crucial as the vibrating intensity. If you are not sure how much girth you want, go smaller rather than larger so you'll know your new toy will fit.

The final criterion to use is your own aesthetic. Say you have whittled the choices down to two or three contenders, and considered all the available information. Now it's time to cast rational thinking aside and pick the one that tickles that sexy part of your imagination. It may be the prettiest one, the kinkiest one, or the most comforting and familiar one. Desire and aesthetic are deeply personal and entwined; so pick the vibrator or vibrators that speak to you.

Lipstick Vibe

or can't come another way, that doesn't make her "addicted" to her vibrator, it makes her a woman who has found a way to have orgasms through vibrator use, the surest way known to get enough direct clitoral stimulation to lead to orgasm. People worry that adding a vibrator to their sex lives is like opening Pandora's Box, and that they will end up regretting reaching for more pleasure. We assure them that in this case Pandora's Box is brimming with fun new sensations and satisfactions, and the only regret they'll have is not opening the box sooner.

Cosmo Vibe

Some of the shyest customers are often the ones who return to the store or write an e-mail that says, "Thank you. I just had my first orgasm at 24 (or 32 or 58). Your store changed my life." Here are some of the main concerns expressed by many a first-time sex toy buyer.

Can I become addicted to my vibrator? This question comes up more often than any other among first-timers. It's folklore, based on sex-negative ideas that sex is only for procreation and not for pleasure, and that too much pleasure can hook you like a bad habit. Not to worry—sex is just another appetite, and appetites find their balance. You will be sated, and you will be hungry again.

Auto Erotic
Single

Some people fear that if they open themselves up to more and more sexual pleasure, it will take over their life. We have found that it's actually quite the opposite. If you don't address your desires, you will spend all your energy keeping them down. Attachment to your new vibrating friend will not lead you to quit your job or neglect your children, but more than likely it will make you more productive and present at everything you do! The truth is that there is no limit to the amount of pleasure you can enjoy.

(For those very few people who suffer from a condition called "sexual addiction," sex toys are not usually the problem. If you think about sex constantly, and find that those thoughts or actions are disrupting your normal life, consult a certified therapist.)

What some people call "vibrator addiction" we see as an orgasmic rut. People are creatures of habit. Most of us in our sexual development find that we like to climax certain ways more than others, or simply find one sure way to climax and do it over and over again. Masturbating can become as rote as brushing your teeth. If you are stuck in

Turtle Vibe

an orgasmic rut, break the habit by varying the ways in which you masturbate and playing with different types of stimulation.

If you are concerned about a vibrator getting in the way of enjoying sex with your partner, take a little time off from it. Put it in a drawer and abstain for a few days, and you'll be primed for your lover's touch.

Honeycomb
Vibe

Will my vibrator desensitize me? Along with the fear of pleasure comes the fear of having it and then losing it. It's reasonable to imagine while feeling the buzzing power of the Magic Wand that it could rub your clit into oblivion—what a terrible fate! But it won't happen. Long sessions of vibration can leave genitals feeling temporarily numb, and as with any sexual activity, you can go at it all day with a vibrator and end up sore. All that means is that you probably won't want to do it the same way the next day. Sensitivity will return, and you'll be back on that pony in no time, no worse for wear.

Fear of dependence on or of damage from a vibrator prevents some women from using

If you are stuck in an orgasmic rut, break the habit by varying the ways in which you masturbate and playing with different types of stimulation.

Care and Feeding of Your Vibrator

Maximize your love affair with that favorite toy by taking good care of it. Be there for it, and it will be there for you.

1. Store the batteries separately from the battery-operated vibrator. Don't just leave them in the toy—you could become a victim of battery corrosion! This goes for traveling, too. Vibrating luggage is alarming to baggage handlers.

2. After use, wash or wipe down your vibrators with warm, soapy water, rinse, and air dry. Be careful not to get the mechanical parts wet, or your vibe will become a paperweight.

3. Use a condom on soft-plastic vibrators for easier cleanup and to put a barrier between you and the material the vibe is made from.

4. Don't share your toy unless you've s wathed it in latex or it's made of silicone.

5. Store your soft-plastic vibes in separate cases in your bureau drawer or toy chest to prevent them from absorbing color from one another.

6. Keep the cord on a plug-in vibe from bending where it attaches to the wand—that's the Achilles heel of the toy, and the reason most Magic Wands eventually die.

7. Freshen up the batteries. If your favorite portable vibe doesn't have the same kick you've come to love, try changing the batteries before giving the toy up for dead.

Trinket Vibe

vibrators at all, and therefore from enjoying the benefits and pleasures of orgasm. The message we give women with vibrator anxiety is that it's okay to want more from your sex life, and to use a vibrator to get it, and it's also okay to put your vibrator aside and open yourself up to trying other things. You are truly in the driver's seat of your sexuality when using a vibrator—it is within your power to pick it up as much as it is within your power to put it back down.

Vibes and Guys

A guy's hands are usually enough to get him off, but who says he can't enjoy the pleasures of vibration, too? Vibrators are well known for their magical orgasmic power for women, but they are by no means a single-sex stimulator. Why not let some of that magic rub off on him?

- Add vibration to the back of your hand during your usual stroke. The Swedish massager, the kind you find at the barbershop, is great for this because it leaves your palm free to do its job.

- Place a vibrator on the perineum to send a buzz toward the prostate, a much-overlooked male erogenous zone. Or go for the full monty and try a buzzing butt plug.

- Plenty of guys get off on vibration on the head of the penis. The Hugger Vibe cups the crown with fluttering plastic flower petals.

- Soup up the Fleshlight, the ultimate masturbation sleeve, by adding a Silver Bullet vibrator. Zoooom!

- Male and female genitals are analogous—what's good for the goose is good for the gander! Try running a vibrator up and down the shaft of the penis and around the scrotum.

Write steamy love letters with the Vibrapen.

Will her vibrator replace me? We hear from a good number of women that their partners don't want them to have a vibrator because it will "spoil them" or otherwise diminish their desire for partner sex. If your partner feels threatened, reassure him or her that no matter how many vibrations per millisecond, how large the dimensions, or how unflagging and powerful the toy, no piece of plastic is a match for human closeness, no vibrator ever said "I love you," and no toy made anyone coffee in the morning.

What a vibrator will do is help a woman come more easily and often—and that kind of sexual empowerment can be life changing and is usually relationship improving.

> **The Pause that Refreshes**

To us, vibrators are right up there with sports bras as brilliant applications of technology to the unique problems of women. While it's true that some men enjoy vibration, primarily vibrators have offered guaranteed orgasms to legions of women. Orgasm is more often a source of giggles on the *Letterman* or *Leno* shows than a serious topic debated on CNN, but we all know that sexual satisfaction is not just a laughing matter. And vibrators enable women to enjoy that satisfaction whenever they want to. Vibrators, we salute you.

Try This: Vibe Tricks

Vibrators don't come with user-friendly operating instructions. In fact, they can be downright confusing, their shapes seeming to conceal their uses rather than making them clear. A classic vibrator, called the Slimline, is a good example. The Slimline is an 8-inch (20cm) long, pointed column of hard plastic. While it can be used to marvelous effect on the clitoris, the Slimline's phallic figure seems to beg for penetration, but using it that way aims the majority of the vibration high up into the vagina—not the area of maximum effect. Often, when a customer first sees the famous Magic Wand, a foot-long massager with a tennis ball—size head, she'll blanch and whisper, "*That* goes inside?!"

No, the Magic Wand wasn't designed to fit inside the vagina, nor does the Slimline have to go there just because it can. The main thing to remember is that you are in charge of the toy, and you can do whatever feels good to you. If you stay open to what your body wants, you can't go wrong! Here are a few tips to help you in your exploration of the world of vibration.

1. Put that suction cup to use! The Wahl 7-in-1 comes with a lot of attachments with no apparent sexual uses, but don't throw out the suction cup. Attach the cup to the vibrator; push the base of any silicone dildo or butt plug onto the cup—and presto! You have the strongest, most reliable vibrating silicone toy in creation.

2. Bring the Magic Wand into your lovemaking. The Magic Wand is smooth and symmetrical, which makes it relatively comfortable to lie down on. Find a comfortable position by using a pillow to prop up the vibe. When your partner enters you from behind, he will feel the vibration through his penis, or she will catch the buzz through her dildo.

3. Take the slow boat. Build up sexual energy by getting close to orgasm, then backing away to intensify the climax. Give yourself enough time with your vibrator, your sweetheart, or both to reach new heights.

4. Fill yourself up with a silicone dildo or butt plug, touch the base with a vibrator, and blast off! Silicone transmits vibration better than any other material.

5. Take it to the streets. A number of our customers acknowledge masturbating outside the home—in a restroom at work, in their cars, in the woods. Vibrators you can wear under your clothes add to the titillation of getting off in new places.

CHAPTER 4

gearing up for getting down

Women are bending their boyfriends over these days with joyful regularity. Recently a vivacious woman walked into one of our stores with her boyfriend. The two of them marched up to the counter, and with her boyfriend smiling behind her, the woman

dildos and strap-ons

declared, "I want to fuck my boyfriend in the ass without spending an arm and a leg!" After much discussion and squeezing of dildos with eyes closed (a better way to gauge the size than just eye-balling it) the pair settled on an inexpensive nylon harness and a great looking silicone dildo, a model called "Mistress."

The stuff dreams are made of: a blowjob at the dildo matinee.

This type of purchase was not always so easy to announce. The first boy-girl couple to come into our store looking for a strap-on was a pair of scraggly young punk rockers, one with hot-pink hair, one with royal purple. Safety pins and patches proclaiming their favorite bands (Fugazi and the Dwarves) held their tattered clothes together. They seemed tough as boot leather. It was only a couple of months after we had opened our doors in 1993, and we were enthralled by just about every customer, and thrilled that we could help them explore their sex lives.

The pink-haired woman let us in on their taboo desire and took the lead picking out the dildo and harness, while her guy, blushing cardinal red, leafed through a magazine. At the register, they took out their money, each paying half of the total. The purple-haired punk flashed us the sweetest smile as he took the shopping bag, and his girlfriend took his hand. They walked out of the store with their purchase, and we knew we had just witnessed something rare and wonderful. We felt like an integral part of the sex toy revolution. We still do, but now it's as likely to be uptown execs bending over as subversive punk rockers.

The Joy of Fucking

There's the primal glee of fucking with abandon, then there's the surge of confident power that comes from giving the ride of a lifetime. Or perhaps it's the spiritual connection of looking deep into your lover's eyes as your hips move together that delights you. Fucking allows us literally inside our lover's bodies, be it with hands, dicks, dildos, or fingers. Not only can penetration be profoundly satisfying emotionally, there are also loads of nerve endings, muscles, and ligaments that come alive in response to that deep, thrusting motion.

The fact that sex is fun is old news, so you won't be surprised to know that dildos have been around for eons. Despite the long history of dildos and the human pursuit of sexual pleasure, these days "good girls" still aren't supposed be sexually aggressive, and "real men" aren't supposed to be anally receptive, so dildos can carry a lot of psychological weight. The deliberate act of buying a dildo to penetrate yourself or your lover takes courage, and like most feats of daring, it's exhilarating. Whether or not gender play is part of the appeal, breaking the rule that penetration is exclusively something that a man does to a woman adds a zing of transgression to the situation and allows for a much fuller range of sexual expression. So when a customer first stands before our wall of dildos, she or he stops reading for a typecast role in the cultural screenplay "How Sex Is Supposed to Be," and starts writing their own script.

Dildos can't make you gay if you're straight, male if you're female, or even good in bed if you're an inattentive partner. No sex act or toy or position can change a person's sexual orientation. But such is the power of the dildo: The mix of desire, fear, and longing that this toy inspires can throw people—even those with stable sexual orientations and gender identities—into a state of panic. The ultra-conservatives hate dildos because they represent pleasure and choice. Don't buy into their puritan mythmaking—release your anxieties, and let your desire be your guide. We're here to help you relax and learn to enjoy!

> No sex act or toy or position can change a person's sexual orientation.

Dildos Are for Everyone

Dykes and sex activists may be the leaders of the modern surge in dildo popularity, but dildos are for everyone. Whether you're a man or a woman, gay or straight, or outside those categories, dildos add another layer of satisfaction to your sex life. Women wear dildos to experience the rush of penetrating their partner. For men who want more size, stamina, or have erectile difficulty, strap-ons are the solution. It may seem strange and perhaps intimidating to wear a dildo, but once over that initial hump of resistance you'll find a lot of new possibilities for intimacy and adventure.

Mistress & Siren

A Brief History of Dildos

Human beings are a creative, industrious bunch. Almost anywhere you look, you can find ample evidence of that creativity being shaped by our basic desire for sex. Reay Tannahill's *Sex in History* notes that a city in ancient Greece about 500 B.C., called Miletus, was the manufacturing center for *olisbos*, or imitation penises, usually made of leather or wood, and anointed with olive oil before use. There is a play dating to the third century B.C. in which two young women argue over a dildo. Dildos are mentioned in ancient erotic texts (the *Arabian Nights* includes an ode to a banana that begins, "O consoler of widows and divorced women.") Handmade phalluses were marketed throughout Europe in the Middle Ages, Italy being a major manufacturing center, according to H. Levin's *American Sex Machines*. The Italians called them *passatempos* or *dilettos*, which evolved into our word, dildo. By the eighteenth century, upper classes had them made by hand from silver or ivory. Ancient Chinese and Japanese cultures embraced the tradition, too. Throughout time and across cultural differences, human ingenuity has served us well when it comes to our desire for sexual fulfillment.

ON YOUR OWN

"If you want something done right ... do it yourself." To bump the intensity up a few notches, incorporate dildos into your self-love life. Aside from the wonderful mood-elevating effects of masturbation, the health benefits of increased blood flow to the genitals, and the muscle-toning bonus of orgasm, self-pleasuring is a chance to be alone with your thoughts and to indulge your fantasies, however decadent or austere they might be. The time we spend masturbating is time well invested in becoming more sexually alive and developing our sexual selves. Masturbation is jokingly derided as the last resort of those who can't get a date, but in reality it is an essential, healthy part of everyone's sexuality.

For women, while it's always fun to "let your fingers do the walking" as you "polish your pearl," a dildo can give you a feeling of fullness that fingers can't quite match. And unless you're a yogi, it's challenging to fuck yourself zealously for very long without pulling a muscle or falling over. Plenty of household objects, from candles and flashlights to fruits and vegetables, have traditionally made fine choices for penetration, but a dildo really does do it better. If penetration is a regular part of your self-love life, a dildo is a wise investment. (The thrill of making salad from your cucumber sex buddy fades after the first few times, no matter how earnest you are about "reduce, reuse, recycle.")

Guys shouldn't feel left out. Men who like penetration can use dildos while they masturbate, too—it's a fine complement to slapping the salami.

BEND OVER BOYFRIENDS AND STRAIGHT CHICKS WITH DICKS

For straight men the anal taboo is shockingly powerful. But many brave men stare down antipleasure taboos in order to have more hot, fun, and exciting sex lives. When we first opened Toys in Babeland, the phenomenon called "bend over boyfriend," or "pegging" (as it is known by readers of *Savage Love*, Dan Savage's irreverent sex advice column) was still underground and considered bizarre by the mainstream, if considered at all. Even gay men who enjoy penetration have faced negative attitudes from within gay circles, despite a generally more supportive subculture. The bottom line is that any man who is willing to be receptive is taking an emo-

---

FAQ

How do I choose?

The sheer number of dildo options can be daunting. The single most important factor is the girth of the toy; so if it's going inside you, choose one similar in size to a penis, cucumber, or number of fingers you've enjoyed previously. If it's for use with multiple partners, get something middle of the road, about an inch and a half (less than 4 cm) in diameter and 6 or 7 inches long (16 to 18 cm).

tional risk—he is setting aside, at least for the moment, the protective armor of the "impenetrable man." So kudos to all you men courageous enough to offer up your ass for penetration! Pleasure will be your reward.

And what fun for the partners of these brave guys! How satisfying to have a man who wants you/it so much that he'll spread his cheeks. Some women may be shocked to find that their male partners want to try ass play, and may even be alarmed by the prospect. Many women grow up expecting to give nothing more than a blowjob, so when suddenly your guy wants you to strap on a dildo and climb on top, it can be a daunting prospect. Just remember:

Wearing a dil doesn't make you any less of a woman. It's simply a chance to step away from the traditional notion that women are exclusively receptive. While being sexually receptive is powerful in its own way, it's fun to mix it up sometimes and see how the other half lives. And the fucker/fuckee dichotomy definitely doesn't correlate to masculinity/femininity. Plenty of feminine women have made a shopping spree out of a trip to Toys in Babeland for sex gear followed by a stop at the cosmetics emporium for lipstick.

A woman in a straight pairing who wants to get in on the strap-on fun may have to do some persuading. Communication, hot talk, and a rosebud massage (see page 105) can help pave the way. Many a woman has seduced her man through the persuasive means of sliding a finger up his ass during a blowjob. Once he experiences direct prostate stimulation, he may become more willing to try other anal activities. There is a pair of encouraging videos (look for the *Bend Over Boyfriend* series) intended to help straight couples who want to enjoy anal play.

Dildos are for straight men, too, who sometimes wear them to satisfy their lovers. Men show self-acceptance and commitment to pleasing their partners by using dildos when they experience trouble getting or maintaining an erection, or when they want to wow their partners with size. For the extra-adventurous straight couple there is at least one strap-on harness that enables a man to wear a dildo while he has a hard-on. That's for "double penetration," meaning simultaneously entering a woman's vagina and anus.

Glitter
Cock

SAPPHIC STRAP-ONS

These days, strap-ons are a common accoutrement of lesbians' sex lives. The thrill of face-to-face fucking while keeping the hands free to roam, plus the opportunity for gender play, makes the strap-on nearly irresistible. Despite the appeal, however, dykes have not always embraced strap-ons. When we started out, strap-ons were controversial among dykes, and many of the dildos sported by lesbians were shaped like dolphins or goddesses, and even the penis-shaped ones were usually lavender.

In a lesbian world now populated by butch/femme couples and drag kings, realistic (penis-shaped) dildos have displaced the marine mammals on our shelves. Many of our lesbian customers, hung over from the sex wars of the 1980s*, have struggled with their desire for a realistic dildo. If they wanted to strap on a dildo that had veins and a head, didn't that mean they wanted to be a man? If a lesbian wanted her girlfriend to fuck her like crazy with a dildo molded from a porn star's

Siren and Bobbie Sue

> ## Herstory
>
> Every year we set up a booth at the Michigan Womyn's Music Festival, a long-standing cultural mecca for lesbians. One year a leathery old dyke dressed cowboy-style visited the booth. In a slow Texas drawl, she told us about how in the 1950s she had desperately wanted a strap-on. She had brought her sketch to a local bridlemaker, but he kicked her out of the shop when he realized what she was after. Desperate, she managed to rig up a harness out of a maxipad holder. (Menstrual technology was a lot more rugged in those days.) That harness, plus a condom carefully packed with cotton, worked as her strap-on for years. She admired our wares and told us, "You gals have things a lot easier than we did." We sure do.

penis, did that mean she was secretly straight? Fortunately, more accepting attitudes and a lighthearted appreciation of the playfulness of sex has freed up dykes to explore their options without the crushing judgment of their sisters.

---

*In a nutshell, the "sex wars of the 1980s" were the bitter debates between feminists who thought pornography was violence against women and those who championed all freedom of speech, including pornography. The "antiporn" feminists often opposed dildos as being too "male," which was a major insult in those days.

TRANS DICKS

For transsexual men, dildos are often extremely important. It doesn't take a dick to make a man, but if you are a man, it's nice to have a dick you feel good about. Unlike their bio-boy counterparts, female-to-male transsexuals (FTMs) get to choose their equipment from a wide range of sizes, colors, and materials. Completely flaccid, soft, and smushy "softpacks" are available to make a perfectly passable package, albeit one you can't fuck with; "Ultraskin" cocks have a texture, shape, and color that make them nearly indistinguishable from nature's version; and silicone dildos offer the durability that a testosterone-crazed horndog needs to save himself from going broke while replacing his equipment.

GOD BLESS GAY SEX!

It might seem as if gay men have plenty of dick already without adding faux phalluses to the mix, but they are often eager and apparently unconflicted dildo users. For solo play, to have a really, really big one, or to perpetrate complicated orgy scenes, dildos are many a happy homosexual's right-hand man. Gay couples we know in which one of the men is HIV-positive prefer a dildo to the risk of exposing the other to the virus. But positive or not, many gay men keep their sex lives rich and exciting by shopping for a new dildo every so often, happily enjoying the variety of sizes and styles available.

Gender Benders

Variously queer and trans "third-gendered" individuals reject the limited scripts that go with the traditional dyad of man and woman. Outwardly defiant, revolutionary gender warriors are leading the political charge, while swaggering butches, mincing drag queens, kinky radical faeries, and regular guys who like to get pegged are creating change through their individual acts of self-expression.

Dildos can be a part of that transgressive defiance. Everybody gets to choose for themselves who they are and fully embrace what they like to do in bed. Most people won't choose to abandon the gender identity of their birth, but everyone can benefit from a little more elbowroom.

Our society asks as its first question "Is it a boy or a girl?" and from that moment on treats the answer as the most important determinant of everything from income to sexual tastes. Refusing to be restricted by society's narrow assumptions about sex and gender opens up a brave new world of possibilities.

What are dildos made of? You name it, and some enterprising soul has made a dildo out of it. We humans have got sex on the brain. From the start, people have created dildos out of the materials at hand, at first carving them from stone, ivory, or wood. These days, manufacturers fashion molds in all kinds of phallic shapes, into which they pour latex, silicone, or the latest synthetic polymers. Some artisans still produce handmade pieces from glass and wood, but the majority of dildos start their lives as thick goo that's popped out of its mold as it hardens.

Silicone is our favorite dildo material.

Silk

Silicone is our favorite dildo material. Silicone has many virtues. It's pliable, but has a firm texture that feels great; it retains body heat, and it's exceptionally durable—well-made silicone toys will last a lifetime. Silicone is non-toxic, and it's also non-porous, thus making it both the safest sex toy material and the easiest to clean.

The first silicone dildos were created in 1971 by Gosnell Duncan who made them from medical-grade silicone for people in the disabled community. Local lesbians got wind of his operation, and soon Sapphic pilgrimages to his Brooklyn studio became common. The gospel of silicone has since spread to the rest of the sex toy world.

Forty years later, that original sculptor is still going strong; he has been joined by many other silicone dildo makers who have greatly increased the variety of shapes and colors available. Most of these craftspeople are sex enthusiasts dedicated to producing a quality product, and silicone dildo making is still a cottage industry that produces the best dildos on the market. Each company's toys have a distinctive texture and palette, as silicone dildo making is a non-standardized process. A few of the big sex toy companies have tried to get into the silicone dil business, but the high-quality manufacturing process hasn't proved profitable for them.

Dildos made from natural materials such as wood and metal also make the grade, as long as they are not finished with some kind of toxic polish. Glass dildos have begun to proliferate in the past few

FAQ

I've heard bad things about breast implants; isn't silicone dangerous?

The silicone used for breast implants is liquid, and if the implant tears, the liquid silicone can get into the bloodstream. Because dildos are solid, there is no such danger.

years, as glassblowers realized they could make thick rods and twists of glass shot through with dazzling color and sell them at sex boutiques. They are gorgeous and a lot easier to produce than stained-glass windows. Glass might seem dangerous, but thick bars of glass are hard to break. They can't be snapped in half with bare hands as if they were sticks of firewood. And if your hands can't break it, neither can your pussy or ass. But if you drop a glass dildo on a hard floor it will shatter. So use common sense, and if your glass dildo has cracks, retire it from active use—it might make a lovely objet d'art instead. Glass, like wood or metal, is too hard to be a good material for a strap-on—you might bruise your partner. Like a flesh-and-blood penis, the best dildos to wear in a harness have some give to them. Hard, curved dildos are fantastic for strong G-spot stimulation, however, and can be used very successfully when held by hand to make a woman ejaculate. With hard toys, be especially careful to scan the surface of the toy before use to make sure it's smooth. Sharp edges or nicks can scratch sensitive tissue.

Most dildos sold in adult shops are made of plastic polymer ("mystery rubber," as sex columnist and educator Fairy Butch calls it), and most of these are pretty unappealing. Oily ooze typically emanates from the cheaper dildos, and it sometimes leaks right through the cardboard of the package. Unless you are looking for a gag gift, avoid these toys.

There is nothing sexy about them, and without a condom those same oils leach off into your body. *Blecch!* There are some other polymers, including Cyberskin and vinyl, that make great-looking and good-feeling toys, but these should also be used with condoms for safety. Research into phthalates (THAY-lates), an unfortunately common additive in many soft plastic polymer or jelly sex toys, suggests that they are potentially harmful, and that they can get into your body through the skin. There is no FDA for sex toys, so we think it's best to err on the side of caution. Besides, condoms make cleanup a breeze.

Dildos range from pinkie size to traffic-cone size. While in a gay store in the Castro district of San Francisco, a friend stepped backwards and fell over a giant dildo that was as tall as Alice in Wonderland's toadstool and as big around as a volleyball. The proprietor assured us that it was not just a joke and was actually meant to be used. We haven't been to that party, but the point is that there is quite a range out there.

Glass dildos (the Cherry Top and a unique hand-blown model) double as objets d'art.

Hand-held Dildos

Any dildo can be used by hand, but some are specially designed for that purpose. As fun and healthy as masturbation is, it can be wearing on wrists and arms. Ergonomic dildos with handles attached make for less of a tendon-tiring reach. G-spots and prostates both respond best to firm pressure, a type of stimulation that is hard to give with a straight, slightly soft dildo.

For self-G or P-stimulation, we recommend the Crystal Wand, an ingenious S-shaped acrylic rod. Slight pressure on the protruding end of the toy causes the other end to rock firmly on the spot. Other hard dildos that are great for masturbation are the Kegelcisor and Betty's Barbell, stainless steel rods designed both for G-spot stimulation and as weights to use for a PC muscle—strengthening vaginal workout. And of course hand-held toys are fun to use with partners, too.

Most dildos are between 4 and 10 inches long, and from $3/4$ of an inch (10–25 cm) to $2^1/2$ inches (2–6 cm) in diameter. The most popular size? About $6^1/2$ inches by $1^1/2$ inches (16 × 4 cm). Although these variations may seem small, even a $1/2$-inch (2.5 cm) difference can feel huge when it comes to the diameter of a dildo. A dildo will lose about an inch of length when you put it in a harness, so for strap-on use you might pick one that's a tad longer than your ideal.

Shapes vary a lot, too. Some people find that the heads of penis-shaped dildos not only make them look realistic but also feel good for the receiver. The heads are often a bit wider than the shaft, with a pronounced lip, which on firmer and thicker dils makes for a satisfying "pop" on its way in and out. Once the fat head is in, the shaft is smooth sailing. Thicker heads are also good for G-spot and prostate stimulation.

Other realistic dildos are tapered, as are most non-realistic dildos. Ripples, ridges, and bumps can stimulate the sensitive nerves around the vaginal opening and add some variety to the in and out. Toys with ripples are popular for anal penetration, as the naturally clenching sphincters happily hug the toy's curves.

Atomic

Champagne Cock

Choosing a Dildo: A Quick Checklist

Faced with a gleaming wall of jewel-colored silicone stallions or clicking through page after page of online selections, it can be hard to know which dil to pick. Use this shopping guide to get a toy you'll enjoy.

- DIAMETER IS EVEN MORE IMPORTANT THAN LENGTH. Choose a dildo with the approximate girth of the number of fingers you like or about the size of a penis you've enjoyed in the past.

- WHEN IN DOUBT, GO SMALLER. Just like the "eyes bigger than stomach" phenomenon that happens at buffets, it's easy to want too much. A toy that's too big is useless, but a toy that's a touch small can still make for a pretty good time.

- IF YOU'VE GOT TO HAVE A BIG ONE. If you want a larger toy, consider a dildo that starts small at the tip and gradually widens in thickness to the base—it will be easier to work in. If the fit is tight, at first only the top portion will comfortably pene-trate, but as the receiver gets more turned on and open, the entire length might slide right in.

- CONSIDER THE ANGLE. Dildos that are curved will arc up and away from the body when worn in a harness. If the dildo is straight, it will aim toward the floorboards, owing both to gravity and to the slightly downward tilt of the pelvis. For that reason, stiff dildos with a curve tend to look better and are a little easier to control (without a hand guiding it to its destination). Curved dildos also give better G-spot and prostate stimulation.

Siren

- REALISTIC OR NOT? If you don't want a toy that looks like a human penis, there is a multi-hued world of rippled forms and miniaturized animals to choose from. If you want veins and balls, those are available, too. Pick a toy that's sexy to you.

- IF YOU'LL BE USING THE TOY IN A HARNESS, get a dildo with a flared, unbendable base; if the base is too small or too soft, it could slip out of the harness.

- TO MOUNT OR NOT TO MOUNT? Some dildos come with suction cup–style bases that allow them to be secured to smooth surfaces, such as tile, for shower or bath-time fun.

- IF YOU CAN'T DECIDE, GET MORE THAN ONE. A major advantage of dildos—they don't get jealous.

There are literally hundreds, if not thousands, of dildos and harnesses out there. The possibilities can be overwhelming. Here are our top recommendations and personal favorites for sexy, high-quality basics.

Harness-Compatible Silicone Dildos

Realistic (penis-shaped) silicone dildos are the best choice for those who want comfort, cleanliness, durability, and realism from their toys. Some of the more realistic toys come complete with balls and a delicate sculpting of veins. Others are more stylized in design. Here are our top picks among them.

Johnny is a large (but not gargantuan), carefully sculpted dick complete with silicone balls. The anatomical detail will appeal to those who want to play with gender. Its pleasing curve makes it good for G-spot stimulation. And it's soft enough to be used for packing, if paired with a jockstrap.

Johnny

Mistress The sleek and slim design of the Mistress nearly begs to be slid up a smooth, tight channel…if you've got one of those (and who doesn't?), this dick's for you.

Leo is the most popular dildo we sell. Its average dimensions ($7^1/8$ by $1^1/2$ inches [18 X 4 cm]) and smooth shape make it appealing to novices and aficionados alike. It's a popular balance between realistic and stylized—retaining some of the features of a penis, like the head and shape, but trading the hyper-real veins for a smoother surface. Its medium-firm texture makes it suitable for both anal and vaginal penetration.

Leo

Non-Realistic Shapes

These provide the physical sensations of penetration without the implications of penis-shaped dildos.

Sirens are gently rippling, rounded toys, each one something like a cucumber with curves. We admire the Siren series for the velvety texture of the silicone and the jewel-like colors.

Sirens

Silks This triumvirate of dils is incredibly sleek and smooth, with rounded tips. Silks, which come in three sizes, are perfect for those who want a smooth in-and-out, uninterrupted by ripples, bumps, veins, or other topographical distractions.

There are also numerous dildos shaped like animals, including dolphins, whales, cats, and dogs. There are even ice cream cones and cowboy boots. If ever you spy one of these unusual shapes and you like it, buy it immediately, as they are hard to find.

Silks 3 and 1

Vibrating Dildos

While some might protest that a vibrating strap-on is gilding the lily, adding vibration is a good way to increase the orgasmic potential of both partners. Vibrating dildos in which the vibration is located toward the middle or base of the shaft allow the buzz to stimulate the first third of the vaginal or anal canal (including the prostate in men). Vibration near the base of a dildo gives thrills to the person wearing the strap-on, too. Vibrations at the tip of a dildo misses the pay dirt of those nerve-rich areas.

Treasure Chest and Bobbie Sue Of the vibrating dildos, our favorites are these two beauties. Both are made of brightly colored,

Bobbie Sue and the Silver Bullet.

firm, resilient silicone.

The base of each dildo is hollowed out to make a perfect little cave into which you can tuck your favorite bullet-shaped vibe. With this setup, the benefits of top-quality (and expensive) silicone are combined with an easily replaceable, inexpensive vibrator. As battery-operated vibrators tend to have short life spans, this arrangement makes sense. The Treasure Chest has a delightfully plump series of ripples, which curve just enough to facilitate G-spot or prostate stimulation. About 2-inches (5cm) wide at the base, it's a little big for a starter dildo, especially for anal sex.

Treasure Chest

The Bobbie Sue is suggestive of a penis in shape, without a lot of detail. More slender and tapered than the Treasure Chest, it's a popular choice for every orifice.

Ruby Ribbed This inexpensive vibrating dildo is made of translucent, bright-red jelly rubber molded around a small Silver Bullet vibrator. Subtle ridges on the shaft give extra stimulation. Unlike its more typical battery-vibe cousins, the Ruby Ribbed has a large base, which makes it usable in a harness.

Ruby Ribbed

"Skin" Dildos

The latest material in dildo manufacture is the uncannily lifelike Cyberskin (also known as Ultraskin or Satinskin). Cyberskin dildos are constructed with the core of the toy made of a thicker-density material than the outer layers. To the touch, it feels like a soft layer of skin over a rigid shaft. With careful attention paid to shape and coloration, the result is an amazingly convincing hard-on. In the dark, it feels so real it's hard to distinguish from the genuine article.

Unfortunately, because of its delicacy as well as overall uncertainty about the safety of the materials, Cyberskin does not get our wholehearted endorsement. It's a mystery rubber, which seems to ooze a bit; careful storing in cornstarch keeps it from getting unpleasantly gooey. Most Cyberskin toys come packaged with a dusting powder to keep them soft but not sticky. Rather than using this talcum powder, which is linked to cervical cancer, dust your Cyberskin toys with cornstarch.

We love Cyberskin for its good looks and sumptuous feel, but it is a high-maintenance material. Cyberskin is porous, so the best way to keep it clean is to use it with a condom. Harnesses can dig into fragile Cyberskin and tear it. The softness of Cyberskin's outer layer renders it very susceptible to changes in shape and color. Shoved into the corner of a drawer, it will gradually mold itself into the shape of the corner, or stored next to a cheap, dyed dildo, it may become stained by the other toy. So Cyberskin toys require careful handling. These are drawbacks, but even so, for realism nothing beats Cyberskin, and if that's what you're after you'll be willing to coddle your Cyberskin cock with all the care this diva of dildos requires. We recommend you always use condoms with Cyberskin and Ultraskin toys.

Ultraskin

Double Dildos

Simultaneous penetration has long been something of a Holy Grail in the world of dyke sex. Lately straight chicks have joined the quest, too. Regrettably, the classic dark-ages double dildo demonstrates a profound disregard for how two bodies fit together. Until recently, all double dildos were long, straight tubes of material molded at each end into the shape of the head of a penis. Rarely were they flexible enough to allow for two people to face each other, each with one end of the dildo in her vagina or anus. Porn movies showed them being used by women ass to ass, playing a sort of sexual Push Me/Pull You. Anyone could see that this was not what most women are looking for when they are seeking to experience penetration at the same time. Fortunately, these extra-long monsters are not the final word in simultaneous penetration.

Nexus Double Dildo

"Togetherness through silicone" is the slogan here, as a new generation of largely lesbian toy manufacturers challenges the big sex toy companies. There is no better example of their success at designing toys that address the real-world mechanics of sex than the Nexus Double Dildo. The intelligent new design has wound up pleasing thousands of lesbians and straight couples alike. Shaped like a modified, uneven boomerang, the Nexus can be worn in a harness or just supported with your hand. Having the same dildo inside you (as the wearer of the strap-on) that you are using on your lover enhances the already potent feeling of connection that comes from fucking. Every movement of the "outie" part of the Nexus is subject to ricochets and echoes through the "innie." The Nexus comes in two sizes and is confected with pretty swirls of color.

Double play: the Nexus Junior double dildo.

Strap-Ons

A "strap-on" is a dildo and a harness put together. In our opinion, the best strap-ons are those in which the harness and the dildo are purchased separately. The one-piece jobs are usually cheaply made, and the flimsy construction won't hold up to the demands of the task at hand—they're like the weaker paper towel in that old television ad. The sturdy two-part setups work because each part is well made; users can choose the style of harness and size of dildo that best suit them. Choosing the two components of your strap-on separately allows you to customize your rig.

Harnesses are usually constructed with a central chassis, which is attached to a waist strap at the top and has either a single G-string–style center strap or two jockstrap-style straps, which wrap around the sides of the butt cheeks. To keep it simple, we call these "one-strap" and "two-strap" harnesses. One-strap harnesses are more like thong underwear—sleek and sexy to look at as well as to wear. The two-strap harnesses offer more genital access. Men need two-strap harnesses, as do women who might want to get fucked while wearing their own strap-on.

All harnesses are built around a hole or a ring that holds the dildo in place. The dildo must have a wide base at the bottom to stop it from slipping right through the hole or the O-ring. Getting a dildo with a base is essential! Some harness rings snap out to accommodate different dildo sizes, which can be very convenient if you have your eye on a thin dildo or one with a smaller than usual base. Harnesses with removable O-rings can also accommodate the fake balls that adorn some realistic dildos.

Get a harness that adjusts easily, and wear it tight, much tighter than you would wear your clothes. Quality harnesses have waist straps that adjust with D-rings or with buckles. D-rings are the double rings that allow you to thread the strap through both rings, then double it back over the top to secure the strap. Buckles are good because they don't slip. D-rings may slip a little, but they are easily tightened again with a quick tug. They're less expensive, too, and as they allow for micro-adjustments, they can fit more precisely than buckled versions. Generally, buckles are best, however, because once buckles are fastened, they stay securely in place.

Unless you're a vegan, the best material for harnesses is leather. Leather is smooth and soft; it warms with skin contact and seems to meld with the body of the wearer. Harnesses come in a variety of other materials as well, including rubber, vinyl, neoprene, nylon, and cotton. Each of these materials has its advantages, except for cotton. If you see a denim harness, run! Anyone who wears jeans knows that denim stretches and loosens as it's worn, and that's great for casual Fridays, but you need your harness to press your dildo securely onto your body for as long as you want it there. Rubber and vinyl harnesses are not as soft as leather, so they are less comfortable to wear, but a harness made of these or other syn-

Buzz Me Tender
One-Strap

Buckling
Terra Firma

thetic materials will not stretch as much as leather, so the fit feels very secure. Harnesses made of nylon webbing are the cheapest, and you can conveniently toss them into the wash with the rest of your laundry.

PSYCHIC DICK

One of the biggest problems that can arise with strap-on sex is the wearer of the dildo feeling alienated from the toy and hence from the sexual experience. On its face, the act of fucking with a dildo doesn't seem to hold much stimulation for the strap-on wearer. It's true that no strap-on phallus has the nerves of the real thing. But it is possible to feel completely connected to the dil as a vital and powerful extension of your sexual self. A useful concept is that of the "psychic dick." Although the dildo is not a flesh-and-blood penis, your desire and excitement as the wearer of the strap-on are as real as anyone else's, and that sexual energy can be channeled through your body into the dildo, and from there into your lover. Think of the dildo as your psychic dick, made manifest.

If you are strapping one on, take some time as you are getting set up to really connect with the toy. Once you have the harness firmly secured, hold the dick in your hand and push the base of it against your body. Feel for a good connection with the sexual energy in your pelvis. Close your eyes and push with your hips into your hand. Visualize the energy running from your shoulder down into your arm and from your body into the dildo. Feel the connection of your hand on the dildo. Notice the sensation of the base pushing into your body. Put a little spit or lube in your hand and slide it around the head of the dick. Try to feel little tremors of delight from soft touches on the head. This kind of preparation can really help you to feel embodied in the dildo.

Penetrating someone is an emotional as well as a physical act, and connecting your own energy to the strap-on helps to open you up to other experiences of deep exchange with your partner.

Plus it makes the sex hotter.

Even with a genuine mental connection to the dildo, the person wearing it may not realize where their dick is at all times. That sets the stage for a wide variety of possible mishaps. The first is the embarrassing situation in which the harness wearer is engaged in a frenzy of humping, only to realize that the dildo has slipped out of his or her lover. Slip-outs occur with penises, too, but the guy usually notices it immediately. Remember that slip-outs happen, and if it happens without your realizing it, don't wither up in embarrassment! Just slide the dildo back in and keep going. A sense of humor and sexual bravery are requirements for fun sex toy play.

Another occasional problem is when a dildo does not move smoothly in and out in synchronicity with its wearer. If the harness is loose, if it's elastic, or if the fuckee has strong muscles gripping the toy, it is possible to pull back and have the dildo stay put, or come lagging after. That makes it pretty hard to get into the transporting rhythm you want to achieve. And thin dildos sometimes wobble a bit if they are slipped through a harness opening that is too wide for them. The dildo can shift around in a way that undermines the feeling of connection you're rooting for.

> A sense of humor and sexual bravery are requirements for fun sex toy play.

Avoid these problems by making sure you get a firm, tight fit between harness and dildo and between strap-on and wearer. Harnesses with removable O-rings solve the wobbly dick problem—just swap out the big O-ring for a smaller one. The tighter the ring encircles the shaft, the more secure the rig will be. The harness itself should have a rock-solid fit to your body. Getting a feel for how the dildo works takes practice. It helps to keep a hand at the base of the toy as you are fucking; holding the base gives a lot of information about where the tip is. With practice and growing familiarity with the strap-on, it'll become easier to know where the dildo is without checking.

There are a number of alternatives to the traditional harness—some will attach a dildo to a bed, a chair, or even a tree; others will attach the dildo to different places on the body. Most notably, there are thigh harnesses, which secure your dick to your strongest limb. These are good for playing horsey on "Daddy's knee," or (at the other end of the kinky spectrum) for those who find the typical strap-on too "male-identified," or those for whom pelvic thrusting triggers bad memories. People with decreased mobility often find a thigh harness easier to use than a traditional strap-on.

Generally, harnesses are presented as "one-size-fits-all" affairs, and just like O/S clothes at the mall, they don't always fit perfectly. If you are small enough that the excess tails of the straps get in your way, just trim them to a better length.

Rock steady: Buckling Terra Firma harness with Bull's Eye dildo.

Some of the harness models—notably the Terra Firma, our favorite—come in a larger size that fits bigger folks. For the supersizers among us, the Crown Harness, which is designed specifically for larger bodies rather than just being the same style cut larger, may be the best choice. Folks carry weight in different ways, so the nylon waist and leg straps of the Crown are extra long, and can be cut down as needed. The waist and O-ring ride up a little higher than with other models so that belly rolls don't get in the way.

Night Rider thigh harness with Silk 2 dildo

Here's a more detailed description of our top choices.

Terra Firma The Terra Firma harness has an exceptionally firm fit to keep that dildo planted, putting to rest concerns about your chosen dick flopping around. This harness quickly shot to the top of our charts, and remains the harness of choice for both newcomers and old hands. It's sleek and simple but has unique features that make it the most versatile harness we sell. Two leg straps and a waist strap snap onto the rubber O-ring that hangs in front of a soft, leather piece covering the pubic mons, or protecting men's natural equipment. The snap-out ring makes it easy to accommodate dildos of varying diameters—for a slender dil just pop in a smaller ring. The leg straps slide along the O-ring to make room for the fake balls that some dildos have. Best of all, like other two-strap harnesses the Terra Firma leaves the genitals open for play. The Terra Firma is available in either leather or nylon. It can be worn right on the pubic bone, or slightly lower to push the base of the dildo into the clitoris of a female wearer.

Joy to the girls: Buzz Me Tender harness with Treasure Chest dildo.

Triangle Harness A simple G-string design makes the Triangle Harness a good choice for women who want to feel more feminine while wearing a dick. That's not an oxymoron—femininity and masculinity come from how you feel about yourself, not from what sex toys you play with. The Triangle won't work for men, but some women report that they get a little clit stimulation from the strap. And with fewer straps and buckles to untangle than two-strap jobs, it's simpler for first-timers to figure out.

Buzz Me Tender Harnesses designed to hold tiny vibrators almost guarantee getting off. The best of these, the Buzz Me Tender, is equipped with a small

pouch strategically placed above the dildo, perfectly situated to vibrate the clitoris of the receiving partner. A second pouch is tucked on the inside of the harness, positioned to put the vibration on the clit of the harness-wearer. Vibration-loving lesbians can enjoy both at one time!

Rubber Harness Equally at home in the steam room or the bedroom, the rugged Rubber Harness is the acme of butch sartorial splendor. The heavy-duty rubber straps and chassis are satisfyingly solid, and the metal buckles and rivets glitter with the promise of a bucking good roll in the hay that will leave both partners dripping and gasping for air. In certain positions the low-cut top of the harness is perfectly placed to graze the clitoris of the receptive partner. The Rubber Harness has an industrial feel owing to its thickness, which causes the edges to dig in a little bit, and the positioning of the buckles right on the ass make it uncomfortable for sitting. So unless you believe that beauty is worth the price of pain, it's not the best harness to wear out for a night on the town.

Butch splendor: the Rubber Harness.

Bionic Harness A variation on the Rubber Harness, a Bionic Harness is the same design rendered in sparkly colored vinyl. A high-femme favorite, the flashiness of this harness is a big fashion leap forward from the low-key black of most harness designs. If strap-ons were considered proper attire for Oscar night, variations on this rig would adorn all the nominees for best actress. Glittering like the coolest banana bicycle seat, pairing this harness with a silver-sparkle dildo will create a look that's as visually stunning as it is powerfully sexy.

What to Do with a Dildo

Intuition and sensitivity (plus some animal aggression) help make for great sex, but be sure to apply what you know about your sweetheart's anatomy. Physically, it's the length and angle of the dildo and the positioning of the bodies that will determine whether an encounter is a ride to remember or a klutzfest consigned to the dustbin of sexual history. Think about creating a feeling of fullness, stimulating the G-spot or the prostate, pleasurable friction, and touching your lover's clit

or penis. Aim for a smooth passage and avoid pressure toward the spine. In any position, wrapping a hand around the base can effectively shorten a too-long dildo.

Get some lube! Lubrication is essential for both vaginal and anal penetration. Some women produce plenty of natural lubrication, but even so, if you want to fuck for very long, it's nice to have some lube. And additional lubrication is a requirement for anal sex. Sexual lubricants are widely available, so there's no excuse for dryness and chafing. Check out the lube chapter for more info.

Get some lube!

Figuring out where the dildo will go once it's inside your lover is easy. While personal taste in sensations varies, basic anatomy does not. A stiff dildo will just plow ahead in the direction the tip is pointing and the body will adjust around it, whereas soft dildos conform to the body's curves. That doesn't mean firm dildos are bad, just that you have to be more careful with them. If you make sure you have a clear path to the good-feeling places (such as the G-spot), firmer toys are great. Because softer dildos easily curve with the body, they are better than stiff ones for anal sex, as the S-curves of the rectum are less likely to be jabbed by a more pliant toy. The anus is also made of more delicate tissue than the vagina, and it doesn't self-lubricate. Lube is necessary, and it's also important not to force anything. Softer toys, plenty of lube, getting thoroughly turned on first, and good communication are the keys to happy butt sex.

Brilliant Cocks

Stiffer toys are easier to control. Folks whose PC muscles are strong enough have been known to send butt plugs flying across the room and to force out dildos with the power of their clenching muscles as they climax. A firmer dildo in a secure harness is less likely to be expelled by such muscular contractions. Finding the perfect degree of pliancy is something of a compromise between comfort and control.

POSITIONS

Fucking with dildos is like dancing: Anyone can do it, but it gets more graceful with practice. It can take a while to find the right position and to learn how to move the toy around, so if it's your first time expect some bumps along the way. Learning what feels good, both as the receiver and the giver, takes some experimentation, so approach it as play—and don't consider it a failure if there is some initial awkwardness.

On a Mission

Face-to-face, belly-to-belly sex can be both incredibly hot and emotionally intense. The intimacy of being able to touch so much skin and look into each other's eyes is part of what makes the so-called missionary position so appealing. For this position, it's best if the dildo angles upward from the wearer's body. The dil will naturally follow the curve of the fuckee's vagina or anus and feel good. If it hangs downward, it may tend to push straight toward the tailbone. That won't feel so good. And if the dil isn't sliding in smoothly it's more likely to pop out.

If you're having a hard time finding a groove in the missionary position, try making some adjustments. Receivers can try bending their knees and putting both feet flat on the bed, which will tilt the pelvis up, making it easier to keep the dildo from popping out. Resting feet or legs on the shoulders of the person sporting the harness also helps. If the one wearing the cock stands on the floor, and bends at the knees to get to the best height, that can make the thrusting easier. Being able to look down and see the dildo sliding in and out can also make it easier for the fucker to see how things are going—and it's a hot visual. If a woman is the receptive partner, the missionary position makes it hard to reach her clit, but if she is lying on a bed, and the dickslinger (you) stands, problem solved. For more clitoral thrills than hands can provide, add a vibrator, either by sliding a vibrating cock ring onto the dildo (check out the Orbit Ring Vibe on

Care and Feeding of Your Dildo and Harness

A little attention to the cleaning and storage of your toys will make them last a lot longer, and will save you from the disappointment of pulling a toy out in the heat of the moment only to find it covered with dust, cat hair, or dried lube.

Here's our quick toy care checklist:

- WASH YOUR DILDOS in hot water and use mild soap between every use. Silicone toys can be boiled to ensure disinfection—a monthly dildo soup (see below) is a fun Sunday-night activity.

- CLEAN LEATHER AND VINYL HARNESSES with a hot, soapy washcloth and towel dry. Don't soak leather. Nylon or fabric harnesses can be machine-washed.

- STORE TOYS IN A WAY THAT MAINTAINS THEIR SHAPE AND COLOR. Toys should lie as flat as possible. Keeping each toy in its own bag will prevent them from staining one another.

- PROTECT THE TOYS FROM NICKS, because tiny cuts will often lead to unstoppable tears.

- KEEP YOUR TOYS AWAY FROM PETS! We can't tell you how many customers report that their dog ate their dildo.

- POWDER "SKIN" TOYS with cornstarch to preserve their soft, fleshy feel. Without cornstarch they get tacky, and that's not so sexy. Don't use talc.

RECIPE FOR DILDO SOUP

Bring a 10-qt. saucepan full of water to a boil. Place silicone dildos and butt plugs into the pot (you might want to use tongs). Boil for 10 minutes, then remove saucepan from heat and allow to cool. When water is no longer too hot to touch, take out the toys and either air or towel dry them.

Use warm water and soap to clean glass dildos.

page 116), using a harness that holds a vibrator (such as the Buzz Me Tender harness), or grabbing a handheld vibe (like a Hitachi or a Fukuoku). To make this position more comfortable you might want to set your bed a little higher off the ground than department stores generally do.

Up the Down Staircase

A nice round ass to bump against, easy control of depth and angle, and a short reach around to the front of the body—it's surprising anyone ever does it any other way. Doggy-style is a great position for both anal and vaginal penetration. If the dildo is short enough that the receiver likes it slid all the way in, this is an especially good position for the one wearing the rig. That sumptuous round rump will bounce back against the fucker and give lots of thudding pressure to the pelvis and genitals. If the receiver gets on all fours you can grab their hips and move them back and forth just the way you like it. Need we say more? You get the picture. Just don't let the bootyliciousness of it all make you forget that the angles of the receiver's parts are reversed from when the receiver is on his or her back. So if the dildo is angled up it heads for the spine, which is uncomfortable. If your dildo is firm and curved, twist it around so that the curve is angled down toward your lover's

navel. If, as the fucker, you can imagine where your partner's prostate or G-spot is, you'll be better prepared to make it feel good for him or her.

Often dildos that fit perfectly in the missionary position will feel too long when you try rear entry. If you experience that problem either try a smaller dildo or wrap your hand around the base of the dick to prevent it from going all the way in. And if you're having anal sex, consider choosing a softer toy.

Ride 'Em, Cowgirl

Straddling your partner as the receiver, whether you're a man or a woman, gives more control over the speed and depth of the penetration. If you're on top, you can lean forward or back to adjust the angle of penetration. From on top you can crouch on your feet and bounce up and down, or kneel and lean back, stimulate your own genitals, do a little show, or keep your face closer to your partner's. This on-top position is often recommended by sexperts to the woman of a straight couple who is trying to reach orgasm during intercourse. From on top she can angle things just so to get the clit action that many women need to come. For more bucking, ask the harness wearer to plant his or her feet flat for leverage, and pump away. They're the pony and you're the cowboy, so enjoy the ride.

Ready for anything: Siren.

How Queer Is That?

If we had a quarter for every time a dyke looking for her first strap-on (often at her girlfriend's urging) asked "What's in it for me?" we'd have enough for a hand-me-down Harley. The dyke blowjob is the ultimate in gender-bending sex theater, because really, what's in it for anyone? The answer is the old truism that our biggest sex organ is between our ears. That's why straight guys can really get off on giving silicone head, too. The point is desire. The idea, the visual thrills, the feeling of power, and the unique physical sensations all combine to make our motors rev.

A person on either side of a strap-on blowjob is putting him or herself out there, so don't be surprised if self-consciousness sets in. If you haven't done it before, you may find yourself thinking something along the lines of "this is weird." Let the thought come up and, like a master of meditation, let it go. You're doing this because it feels good to you, sucking that thick cock in your mouth, or watching your lover's head bob diligently up and down your shaft. Get into the perverse thrill, and when you've both come like crazy, give yourselves a pat on the back for being brave. It ain't easy being a sex freak (but at least it's not lonely).

Ad Infinitum

Side by side, sitting, standing—the variety of positions is limited only by your imagination and flexibility. Some folks want to sweat the night away in one long, slow groove, while others like to change positions as frequently as partners at a hoedown. Fortunately, it's easy to flow from one position to the next as the mood changes. As you dosey-doe, keeping in mind the alignment of anatomy and dildo will help you avoid any awkward moments.

Buried pleasure: the Treasure Chest dildo holds any bullet-shaped vibrator.

Strap-on Blowjobs

Giving a strap-on a blowjob is both a psychological and physical art. Silicone dils are somewhat lacking in the nerve-ending department, but what is lacking physically you make up for with imagination and enthusiasm. For your next session of "swallow the sausage," here are some tips from both sides of the harness to make the scene go down easy. Many of these work with real cocks, too!

- **Use a realistic cock.** Blowjobs are no time to surprise your sweetie with one of those lavender dolphin dildos from the '80s, cute as they are.

For decent dick sucking you need a sexy number with a clearly defined shaft and head (maybe with a pee slit, too), and veins and balls if possible. When you strap on the dick, take a few moments of private time to really connect with it. Touch it, rub it; if you're packing, enjoy the feel of it pressing against your pants. Make sure that the base of the cock is right where it feels most solidly connected to your body.

- **Think psychic dick**. Although it's not a flesh-and-blood penis, your mind can have a hard-on that's as raging as anyone else's. The dildo is the physical expression of a mental and emotional reality, and that dick can feel fantastic, rubber or not.

- **Do it somewhere nasty**. Something about cocksucking calls for dark alleys, bathroom stalls, and parked cars. Let the staging add to the sexiness.

- **Put on a good visual show**. When you're sucking, remember that your playmate is getting off largely on imagination and the look of your hands, mouth, tongue, and head. So make sure there are good sight lines and keep your actions visible.

- **Use your hand** to push the base of the dick into the blowjob receiver's pelvis. The most physical sensation for the receiver comes from that one point of contact, so make it work. Rhythmically thrusting with your hand along the shaft into the base while working the head in and out of your mouth gives both a visual and a physical thrill. Another good reason to hang on to the base of the dildo is to control the depth of the thrusts.

- **If you can deep throat, do it**. No matter what anyone's gender, deep throating is always impressive and exciting. Avoid jaw pain and headaches—we can't unhinge our jaws like a snake, so find something reasonable to wrap your lips around.

- **Treat the dildo like a real penis**. Focus on the things that feel good to bio-men: Stroke the vein along the bottom, tongue the slit, and gently tickle the balls.

- **If you like using condoms** to keep the dildo clean, this is a great opportunity to show off that safe-sex trick in which you roll the condom on with your mouth.

- **A finger in the ass** is a potentially mind-blowing blowjob complement for receivers of any gender. As for other orifices, while one blowee might not mind if you slip some fingers in her pussy while you're blowing her, another might find that upsets her mental gender-bending state. So check in before adding any penetration.

Mr. Big

TAKING IT TO THE STREETS: PACKING

"Packing" means wearing a dildo under your clothes out into the world. It's called packing because you've got to arrange the equipment carefully to make a nice-looking package. Sometimes the goal of packing is to pass as a man. That goal usually calls for "packing soft," meaning to create a bulge in your pants that looks like a non-erect penis. To pass as real, the package must be fairly discreet. Dildos that are used for sex are usually too big and erect, and look like a salami stuffed in your jeans. Until a few years ago, there was a lively discussion among FTMs and others about how to make the best soft package—one widely touted method involved rolling up hair gel in nylons. The result was a comfortable, stable, and realistically mushy bulge.

These days, drag kings, butches, and transgender men need no longer invest in uncharacteristic purchases of Dep and L'Eggs, because soft, completely flaccid Cyberskin dildos are now manufactured just for packing. Available in several sizes and skin tones, Soft Packs (a.k.a. "packers" or "packies") are much easier to manage than the old-fashioned contraptions, and they make a nice silhouette if your jeans are tight enough.

Mighty real:
Soft Pack dildo.

Other times the goal of packing is to be ready to fuck at a moment's notice. Packing a dick that's usable for sex, or "packing hard," can pose something of a challenge. If it's big enough to penetrate, it usually makes a prominent lump. And it's not that sexy to re-create the classic awkward "tent-pole" of a 13-year-old boy. A few dildos that are up to the task of penetration are also soft enough to bend if

Give the Clit a Piece of the Action

As an alternative to a strap-on dildo, some adventurous women like to turn their clits into cocks. You'll need a high-quality nipple pump, fashioned with a detachable cylinder. Use the pump to pull the clit into the cylinder, thus enlarging it and creating a pleasurable feeling of suction. Detach the cylinder from the hose and pump, leaving it on your engorged clit. Next take a cybersleeve (a hollowed-out penis extension that has a firm tip and semi-thin sides) and roll it over the cylinder. You can secure the sleeve with a cock ring. You now have a realistic dick, complete with sensation from the suction caused by the cylinder. Imagine jerking off or receiving a blowjob on your new dick when you can actually feel the tugging and subtle moves of your partner's hands and mouth! Thanks to Sex Educator Brandie Taylor for sharing this innovation with us.

Red Licorice

stuffed into tight-fitting underwear. A jockstrap offers more industrial-strength control for wearing one of the bigger boys out. It's like a girdle for butches—it battles the bulge. A discerning eye will still notice, but it's amazing how seldom women get their crotches cruised. If "busted" by a perceptive stranger who looks askance, just smile and carry on. Hopefully, the delight of your date will make up for any embarrassment suffered.

Dildo mania

Ain't dildos great? Now that you know the basics of strap-ons and dildos, you'll find that you can do all sorts of things you couldn't do before. Whether it's fucking your boyfriend, double penetration, fucking your girlfriend, taking something bigger than any God-given penis, or just stuffing your pants and giving onlookers something to wonder about, dildos will allow you to experience more of what life has to offer.

Try This

With your harness strapped on tight and a willing partner primed and pleading for penetration, you're ready to start fucking in earnest. Here's how:

1. Slick lube up and down the shaft of the dildo.

2. Use your fingers to put some juice on your lover's orifice of choice. Take the opportunity to rub and massage the opening while you're there—a sexy little greeting and promise of what's to come.

3. Switch the stimulation from your fingertips to the head of your dildo. Grasping the dildo firmly around the shaft so you can easily control the force and depth, gently push it into the hole.

4. Start by fucking the opening, just using the tip of your toy. Watch your partner's responses—as the pleasure mounts, you'll see his or her hips rise to meet you. Then they may be ready to take more inside, so you can go deeper.

5. Keep it up, and soon you'll be in to the hilt!

butt, butt, butt

It was a regular day at the New York City store. As a couple of shoppers wandered around, talk among the Sex Educators turned to lunch. Suddenly, a thickset man sporting a crew cut and dressed in a trench coat walked in, stepped with authority up to the counter, flipped out a police badge,

anal toys

and said, "I'm Detective Smith. The bodega around the corner was just robbed."

"Oh! I was just there!" exclaimed one Sex Educator. "I didn't see anything—I must have just missed it!"

The detective told us the details of the robbery, gave us a description of the suspected perpetrators, and asked us questions. Despite feeling badly for our neighbors, we couldn't help but be a little enthralled by the investigator. We'd had beat cops in before many times, but never a detective! Being expert fantasists, we imagined him in hot pursuit, running through the back alleys, tackling the guy that ripped off our neighbors, pulling him up by the lapels and barking something like, "That's all she wrote, pal. We're going downtown."

Bumper crop: Objects in photo may appear larger than actual size!

As he finished taking notes, we noticed that his eyes were roaming over the lube display. He fingered the little pouches and casually said, "On another topic, I'm trying to have anal sex with my wife."

Full stop. Huh? It wasn't that we didn't counsel people from all walks of life every day about anal sex, but now? During the investigation? We came to. This wasn't television, it was Toys in Babeland. "Uh, of course you are. Yeah, that's a common thing to do. What's the problem?"

He confided to us that he didn't know whether he was doing something wrong, or if perhaps he and his wife just weren't compatible. We gave him a short course in anal dos and don'ts, picked out some lube, encouraged him to listen to his wife and share his feelings, and handed him our anal sex tip sheet.

As the transaction concluded he said, "Back to police work. You gals be careful. Look out for a sedan with South Carolina plates, and call me if you see any-thing." He handed us his card and walked out, lube in hand.

Free Your Ass and Your Mind Will Follow

Intense sexual gratification is the number one reason people have anal sex. Anal sex can send the turn-on meter through the roof. That often-overlooked universal hole can be as full of thrills and excitement as its genital neighbors. Just as with the clit, labia, cock, and balls, arousal floods the anal region with blood, causing the asshole to plump up in anticipation of pleasurable touch. This is not news to a lot of people—at least those lucky ones who already enjoy this highly sensitive erogenous zone. For many others, however, the anus—despite sitting there so close to all the other delectable sex bits—has been ignored. But that's changing, as the anus finally seems to have come to popular attention in all its sexual possibility.

Anal sex can send the turn-on meter through the roof.

Fears and anxieties abound when it comes to anal sex. At worst, this supersensitive erogenous zone gets stigmatized as dirty and perverse; at best, it's just thoughtlessly neglected as a legitimate spot for sexual play. In the absence of accurate information about the anus and the rectum, and a lack of support and understanding for people's desire for anal sex, misconceptions and myths loom large. People believe all sorts of nonsense—that anal sex must be painful, that butt-sex practitioners all end up unable to control their bowels. It is widely believed that women

Sphincter pleaser: Sweetie silicone butt toy.

have anal sex only to please their boyfriends, and that straight men who want it are secretly gay. With such an array of misunderstandings at work against anal pleasure, it's a wonder that the little orifice next door ever gets its day in the sun.

Getting Past the Anal Taboo

Cultural norms suggest that we're not supposed to get any pleasure from our assholes. Owing to feelings of shame we may have experienced during the toilet training years, and the urgent homophobic warnings men receive throughout life, most people learn to ignore their assholes. We turn our attention elsewhere, and except for a few moments a day, may forget entirely that we even have an asshole. But those in the know recognize that the anus is awesome! For men, it's the gateway to prostate stimulation, and for women it's something of a secret pathway to G-spot stimulation. Try a new approach: Spend a little time thinking of your asshole as a beautiful rosebud of pleasure, because that is what it can be.

Spend a little time thinking of your asshole as a beautiful rosebud of pleasure, because that is what it can be.

The Brilliant butt plug is a classic.

Become Friends with Your Butthole

If you've never explored anal pleasure before, you have an exciting adventure ahead. The first thing to do is pay more attention to the state of your anus. A lot of us live with chronic anal tension. Without any conscious effort, we keep the external sphincter of our anuses squinched as tight as can be. Check in with your own asshole now. Just move your attention to your anus, and notice what's going on with it. If you feel tension, tell yourself to relax. Feel your asshole softening. There is no need to sit tightly, because the internal sphincter does a fine job of preventing any fecal matter from sliding out. At worst, chronic anal tension can lead to health problems. At best, it is an unnecessary block to sensual pleasure.

Anal sex can be deeply pleasurable and entirely without pain. Pain arises from forcing something past a clenched, unwilling asshole. As you become more acquainted with your asshole and its states of being, you'll be able to relax the anal sphincter at will, and to enjoy penetration. However, you needn't be in such a hurry for anal penetration that you miss out on the joys of more subtle anal stimulation.

Check in with your own asshole now.

Toys in Babeland has a simple, enjoyable program for getting in touch with your anus. First, get into the habit of checking in with it. Try some anally focused Kegel exercises, clenching and unclenching your sphincter muscles. Anal Kegels can be done in sets of 12; try doing a fast set and a slow set. During the slow set, exhale on the relaxation portion of the exercise. The beauty of Kegels is that no one can tell you're doing them, so they're fun to do in boring meetings, at red lights, and so on. But it's also helpful to do them occasionally when you are in a quiet, private space and can pay deep attention to your body.

Don't be shy about touching your asshole. In the shower, when you're already naked and clean, ease a soapy fingertip just slightly into your ass. Feel around the outside of the hole. Do some clenches and releases while touching yourself so that you can feel the changes in your asshole. Try rubbing in tiny, concentric circles around the rim of your asshole. Notice whether there are any particularly sensitive spots. Don't feel that you have to go very far inside. Just explore and enjoy yourself. For some people external touching is the most satisfying type of anal pleasure. As you become more comfortable with your anus, you may find that paying attention to it yields a variety of benefits. Releasing anal tension is a good way to relieve stress—much like a shoulder rub! And easier and more regular bowel movements may be a positive side effect of your sexploration.

All of this physical exploration will help dissolve the psychological barriers. As you replace your fears with pleasurable experiences you'll soon be able to laugh off the idea that anal play is dirty, wrong, or painful.

FEELING NO PAIN

Anal sex should not hurt, not even a little bit. It's commonly thought that pain is an ordinary part of anal sex. It isn't. Sharp pain upon entry is a sign that your sphincters are not relaxed and open. Many people, especially women, go past this point and endure the pain only to ultimately reject anal sex because of the unpleasantness of the experience. Pain is not something to push through; it is your body or your lover's body telling you to slow down or to try again another time.

Never use desensitizing or numbing products or lubes with numbing agents in them. These products (Anal-Eze is one example) disable our bodies' valuable warning system. If you are numb, you won't be able to tell if you are doing damage to yourself, and on top of that, you can't feel the pleasures that anal sex can bring. Prolong is the same as Anal-Eze, except in slightly different packaging. Prolong is marketed as a desensitizing cream to help men postpone ejaculating, but it has a deadening effect on everything it touches. It makes sense to stay away from any sex products that promise to knock out your sensitivity.

Try rubbing in tiny, concentric circles around the rim of your asshole.

CLEAN IT UP

Cleanliness is nice for all sexual activities, but the anus is the final gate of our digestive tract, so it is particularly important to practice good hygiene when partaking of anal pleasures. Start with a shower, but remember that external washing does not always prevent an encounter with a speck of fecal matter, particularly in penetrative anal sex. For many, a little poo is not the end of the world. But for others it is a deal-breaker, the one and only reason that they refuse to explore anal sex. Getting past this drawback is worth it. Most anal sex does not involve going any farther than the rectum, which is the chute that fecal matter passes through on its way out and in which usually not more than a trace remains. Still, nothing short of douching will guarantee a completely poop-free adventure. If you don't want to douche (or even if you do), using a latex barrier such as a condom or a glove will prevent any infelicitous matter from touching hands, dicks, or toys.

The Greatest Love of All: Anal Masturbation

We masturbators rub our clits, our penises, and our balls—we use vibrators, hands, and lube. Those of us with pussies may push and pull with our favorite dildo until we see stars. The anus is waiting to be invited to this party. Remember, you have nothing to lose and everything to gain from becoming the best masturbator you can be.

Another benefit of masturbation (yes, there are more!) is that it allows us to discover what we like sexually in private. If we want to, later we can share our discoveries with our partners. Stimulating your own ass is a great way to prepare to have partner sex that includes your anus, and, if you are encouraging your partner to offer you his or her ass, to find out exactly what you are asking for.

> Remember, you have nothing to lose and everything to gain from becoming the best masturbator you can be.

Butt First: The Anal Douche

An anal douche squirts water into the rectum to flush out any traces of your last bowel movement. Less elaborate than a full enema but more complete than a soapy finger in the shower, it's a fastidious anal-sex lover's dream accessory. Filling and emptying the rectum a couple of times with comfortably warm water clears the path for mess-free fun. Caution: Douche a couple of hours before you intend to have anal sex to give the good mucous that coats the rectal walls time to return.

Anal Douche

Do Women Really Like It?

Yes, many of us love it, and here's why. In part it's fun because anal play is a little bit naughty, and many women enjoy playing at being bad. But primarily there are sound physiological reasons why anal penetration feels good to women. All the sensitive nerves, orgasmic muscles, and engorging flesh of the sex organs surround and include the asshole. The little ripple of labia on the back of the vagina (called the fourchette), the perineum, and the external anal area are all very sensitive to the touch. Inside the body, the anal canal lies right next to the vagina, and the wall that separates them is very thin. Thus anal penetration can stimulate the G-spot through the wall of the rectum. Because the G-spot responds primarily to pressure, firm touch through the anal walls is just as effective as it is through the vaginal walls. It feels different, though, because anal penetration necessarily hits all those anal nerves on the way. The anal sphincter's opening is tighter than the vagina's, and penetration can feel more intense.

Darling

Bend Over Boyfriend

From our perch behind the counter at Toys in Babeland, we have had the supreme joy of seeing a burgeoning trend of straight couples shopping for dildos and harnesses. This phenomenon—guys bending over and enjoying anal penetration from their girlfriends—shakes the foundation of our society's most basic assumptions about gender and sexuality. (It bears repeating that playing with gender roles is part of what these heterosexual couples find so alluring about dildo and harness play, but there is not a sex toy in the world nor a sex position in all of creation that can make a straight man gay or turn any woman into a man.) A quiet revolution is taking place in bedrooms across North America—women are strapping on cocks and their men are embracing the power of receiving.

Women are strapping on cocks and their men are embracing the power of receiving.

What can a man expect from this kind of sex? Direct prostate stimulation is one reward for trying anal penetration. Our male customers tell us that prostate stimulation feels a lot like G-spot stimulation for a woman—and G-spot stimulation provides an intense, whole-pelvis thrill that many women crave. Sexperts and sexplorateurs agree that men who go through life without trying direct prostate stimulation are missing out on a truly mind-blowing sexual experience. A man may end up not loving the feeling, but he owes it to himself to try it at least once.

Occasionally, a man may lose his erection during anal penetration. Some men report that they deflate because they are focusing so intently on their asses during penetration that all else falls by the wayside. Others claim that to maximize their pleasure, they relax so completely that they go limp all over. Knowing this gives some men pause. Just remember,

you don't have to have a raging hard-on to have spectacular sexual sensations. There are loads of sexual experiences awaiting you that have nothing to do with your erect penis.

The message is clear—it is okay to want anal sex.

What's in it for the woman who straps it on? Time after time we have watched a woman in a heterosexual pair light up as she tries on her first dildo and harness. No more wondering about the experience of an erection—now she has one of her very own to play with. At first, some women find it unsettling to try on the power of penetration, but a woman feeling powerful wearing a dildo is still a woman feeling powerful, and it takes nothing away from the power of her pussy. In fact, it only adds to the varieties of sexual power she can feel—adds another tool to her shelf of sexual creativity.

Diamond Lil Plug

10 Reasons to Try Butt Sex

1. A whole lot of people swear it feels great.

2. It is part of your genitals, and you owe it to yourself to explore it.

3. There is no pain involved.

4. Variety is the spice of sex.

5. Guys: It's the only route to your very own G-spot.

6. Women: It's another route to yours.

7. Closed-minded bigots think it's a sin, so it must be fun.

8. Your anus is a part of yourself you can choose to enjoy.

9. Sex is a playground for adults, and every ride has something to offer.

10. Why not?

What to Do with a Butt Toy

As with any erotic activity, a little knowledge can transform pretty good sex into outstanding sex. Relaxation is the key ingredient in satisfying anal sex play, and to relax, we've got to alleviate our concerns. The message is clear—it is okay to want anal sex no matter what your gender or sexual orientation, and there is no reason to deny yourself the pleasure it has to offer. Here are some guidelines to follow for safe and sumptuous anal stimulation.

TOYS YOU WERE BORN WITH

We like to tell our customers that they were already born with some of the best anal toys available—their tongues and fingers. Nothing on earth feels like a tongue on your anus. At first blush, analingus, or rimming, may not sound appetizing or even remotely sexy. But kissing such a private part of a lover's body is an intimate and erotic act. The anus is so sensitive it practically begs for attention from the muscular yet delicate tongue. (Sometimes its owner does beg!) A clean, winking little asshole is a perfect target for a passionate, French kiss.

> **Nothing on earth feels like a tongue on your anus.**

Latex barriers also come in handy for rimming, and are recommended for risk-free analingus. A superthin Glyde dam or even plain old plastic cling wrap with lube on the receiver's side takes care of most people's reservations about giving their lover's asshole a good tongue-lashing, and still preserves much of the sensation for the receiver.

Fingers make excellent butt toys. You might want to try is adding a finger during oral sex. Just slide a well-lubed pinky a little way into your lover's anus, then watch your lover's back arch and toes curl—it's a quick way to spice up going down.

Fingers also can serve as scouts for a bigger mission. Touching your partner inside and out helps relax and ease the asshole into enjoying penetration, while helping you get a mental map of where to aim the toys or penis you may want to introduce later. Fingers are the only instruments for fucking some folks ever need. Nothing moves quite like them. A beckoning "come here" motion toward the front wall of the rectum hits the prostate in men and indirectly stimulates the G-spot in women. The feeling of your lover's asshole clenching and fluttering around your fingers during orgasm is a pearl beyond price.

> **The feeling of your lover's asshole clenching and fluttering around your fingers during orgasm is a pearl beyond price.**

Once you've both agreed to penetration, start slowly. The receiver gets to set the pace. Fingers, small toys, lube (and love) are all great for warming up and helping to relax and open the sphincter. Start with one finger; when your partner says it feels good, go to two. If you want to penetrate with your cock, go very slowly with your penis or dildo, and don't forget: The receiver gets to say how deep it goes. Your partner may need to get used to the feeling of penetration before being ready for any pumping. For a woman, a vibrator on the clit can increase her level of arousal and help to make the penetration feel erotic. Some preliminary orgasms before you go for initial anal penetration won't hurt—and they help relax all the muscles in the area.

> **The receiver gets to say how deep it goes.**

Glyde Dam

Field Guide to Butt Toys

Anal toys come in a few time-honored shapes that the willing butt cannot resist. The most famous is the "butt plug." The raison d'être of this plug is to give the ass stimulation while freeing the hands for other things. The archetypal butt plug is shaped like a spade, or a miniature lava lamp. The tapered end initially opens the butthole; as it is gently inserted, the widening body of the toy gradually opens the sphincters. Once the widest point of the toy is past the guardian sphincters, they close around the neck of the plug, and voilà, the butt is plugged. Butt plugs have a flared base to keep them from disappearing into the rectum. Because of its clever shape, the plug stays put once it's popped in. In addition to the feeling of pressure that many people find pleasing, the anal sphincters reflexively close on the neck of the plug. Finding something there, they open again, then reflexively close. That little pulsing cycle of sphincter clench and release stimulates the ass, too.

Beginners often choose slender plugs, which seems to make sense, but unfortunately, thin plugs have a tendency to slide back out, especially at the moment of orgasm or if left in for a long time. That kind of minor misadventure just comes with the territory—as your butt gets more experienced, it will accommodate the wider-body plugs that really stay put.

If anal fucking is the goal, the prerequisite is a good, long warm-up. Enter the butt plug. A simple butt plug can relax sphincter muscles and open them

Butter Up for Butt Toys and Other Tips

- Anything going in the ass should be clean, so wash up. The rectal walls are thin and absorbent. A good rule of thumb: don't put anything in your ass (or your pussy) that you wouldn't put in your mouth. Latex gloves take care of any roughness on the hands, and they're the cleanest things around, so consider using gloves if you're planning an anal handjob.

- Using a condom or a glove on the toys, penis, or hand is hygienic and makes for quick cleanup.

- Anything that has been inside the ass should not go in the pussy until it's been thoroughly cleaned. That's why latex is so helpful—you can have sex up the ass, then whip off the latex barrier before touching the pussy.

- Anal sexpert Tristan Taormino recommends using unscented baby wipes to catch lube that threatens to travel south from the ass toward the vagina, a mix to avoid. Designed for delicate baby parts, these wipes won't harm adult genitals either.

- Using a black condom or darker-color toys can prevent getting an inadvertent or unwanted look at any mess.

Midnight Desire Condom

up for later penetration with a dildo or penis, leaving your hands free to roam around pleasing the rest of your lover's body while her or his ass gets ready.

Pendant The Pendant is the perfect beginner's plug. It's one of a lovely family of butt plugs we import from a small company in New Zealand. The jewel-colored silicone is mixed in eye-candy swirls and then sculpted into several well-thought-out shapes. The

A dynamic trio: Pendant, Buddy, and Tristan silicone butt plugs.

Pendant's conical pyramid gently tapers to a modest bulge; from there it cinches to a small neck and swells back out to form the final oval base of the toy.

Buddy is the butt plug that exemplifies everything you would want in a first (or maybe a second) plug. Made of silicone, Buddy is smooth, relatively small, and easy to clean. Its tip is small enough to put the first-timer at ease, and its curve when facing forward follows the natural curve of the rectum. After its sweet and easy beginning, Buddy bulges out, challenging the anus to open further. Don't push it if it hurts. Once it does slide in, the anal sphincters' strong bands of muscle will relax into a new shape around the toy.

Tristan Plug In response to a common plea, "Give me a silicone butt plug that actually stays in my ass!" Tristan Taormino designed this namesake toy with a generous head and a skinny neck. The contrast allows the sphincters to close around the neck and keep the plug in place. An intermediate-level toy, the Tristan Plug's head is bigger than most first-time butt-plug users can accommodate, but for those with a few notches in their belts, it's a favorite.

Size Matters

Some people find that their taste in plugs grows quickly from the smaller to the more moderate. A relatively small plug may not create the same intense sensations for long. The butthole has a physical memory and becomes less resistant to entry after practice. A small plug will likely stay in only at the beginning of your anal explorations, before your anus gets used to penetration and learns to relax. This "expanding butthole" phenomenon is not infinite—after learning to release a lifetime of habitual anal tension, most folks find medium-size plugs suit them just fine. For those who like to push their limits, bigger (and still bigger) plugs are available.

Rosebud We first spotted these exquisite European plugs in the Musée de Sexe in Paris. A museum seemed a fitting home for these sleekly beautiful plugs, but fortunately they are available for private bedroom collections, too. Crafted of stainless steel and polished to a highly reflective sheen, each heavy plug starts with a dulled point and swells to an aesthetically and sensually pleasing bulge, then narrows back down to a long, slender neck. The bases are adorned with either beads of smooth or cut glass, or sculpted brass flowers. The plugs are pleasantly heavy, and they sink easily into the ass of a recipient lying on his or her belly. Once in place, the metal warms up with body heat and the plug is surprisingly comfortable to wear. They're smaller than the Tristan Plugs, but stay in place because of the good design of their necks.

Jewels fit for a queen (or a king!): Red, Flower, and Crystal Rosebud plugs.

Zippy vibe with Zing plug

VIBRATING PLUGS

As if all that wasn't enough, some plugs vibrate, too. The vibration travels through the plug to stimulate the prostate for guys and the deeper structures around the clitoris in women. Vibration can also help the anus to relax a bit, so sometimes it's possible to enjoy a vibrating plug that's slightly bigger than you could handle otherwise.

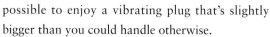

Tulip Plug The curved, pudgy contours of the velvety-soft Tulip Plug practically guarantee anal delight. A gently tapered tip quickly widens to a golf ball–size body, but unlike a golf ball, the material of this plug is quite soft and pliable. Encased within the thick Cyberskin sheath is a small bullet vibrator. As wonderful as this plug feels without the vibrator activated, the earth really starts to move when the adjustable speed control is turned on. Cyberskin is probably the most comfortable material a plug could be made from, and the thin neck on this toy makes it even more stable and enjoyable. The surface of the plug gives a bit, as human flesh does, so they feel good together. If you have a yen to test your limits by wearing a plug in public, this is the one we recommend—but with the vibe turned off. With that demanding buzz thrilling your behind, there is no way to maintain even a semblance of composure.

Tulip Plug Vibe

ANAL BEADS AND BEAD TOYS

Another group of plugs is based on the sphincter-pleasing qualities of anal beads. Anal beads, and toys fashioned after them, are unmatched for anal delight. Simple anal beads are a series of small balls strung together and spaced an inch or so apart on a nylon string. As each ball enters the anus, it provides the sphincter with the pleasing feeling of sliding open, engulfing the little ball and closing shut behind it.

Anal Beads Five balls on a string mean five exciting openings of the anal sphincters on the way in. Once inside, the balls bunch up to create a pleasant feeling of pressure—and they feel even better on the way out. If you get the basic set of hard-plastic beads (a well-spent five bucks), check the beads for sharp seams and make sure the knots are secure. If you find any rough spots, smooth them down with a nail file of fine sandpaper.

Some of the fancier sets of beads are not actually strung up per se, but are placed on a flexible stalk that is made of the same material as the beads themselves. Some of our favorites of these are either graduated in size—starting small, with each successive bead larger than the last—or else form a two-ended stalk with smaller-size beads on one end and larger ones on the other.

Whichever type you choose, the thrill is not just in putting the beads in. Pulling the beads out, either during orgasm or perhaps to incite orgasm, offers an incredible

Ripple and
Blue Beads

rush. As each beads pops out, the body hasn't quite finished processing the sensation of the previous bead, and the pleasurable nerve-firings pile up on one another in a tumbling cascade that boosts an already dynamic sensation right over the top.

If you plan to reuse your toys, look for a set that is easy to clean. The nylon strings of the cheapest beads are hard to clean, so it may be easier just to toss them after use. Another possibility is sheathing the beads in a condom before or as they go in.

Ripple A silicone plug in gorgeous, iridescent midnight purple, with the shape of graduated beads on a thick stalk terminating in a wide base, the Ripple combines the sphincter-pleasing aspects of beads with some of the staying power of a plug. Ripple 1 is great for beginners, and Ripple 2 is for those ready for the next level. Hold the base in your hand and slide it in and out for a hand-held ride that'll curl your toes, or just pop it in place and move on to other activities.

Jewel is an anal-play toy from New Zealand that come in something of the shape of a little Christmas tree. A softly pointed top slides down to the first ripple, where the plug tucks in to start the beginning of a second ripple, and so on, to a total of four bumps. Each ripple has a bead-like effect—the sphincter has the pleasure of opening and closing around each silicone bump as it goes in. It feels twice as good coming out.

Adventurer An eggplant-colored, vinyl-sheathed anal vibrator, the Adventurer looks like a simple anal probe but is so much more. Its slightly bulbous tip and rippled contour are a butthole's delight. As a bonus, the controls not only turn on the vibration but also start the shaft twirling in circles. For most anal-sex lovers, a little motion in the ass goes a long way toward erotic ecstasy. The Adventurer's vibration and swinging motion up the ante and can become the overriding sensation, no matter what else is going on.

DILDOS FOR THE BUTT

"Relaxation, communication, and lubrication" is our butt-sex mantra. Make sure you tag each of these bases before you slide on home! Before jumping in with a dildo, warm up the ass with external touching, finger penetration, and maybe some toys. If you're having sex with a partner (as opposed to masturbating), keep communicating as you go. Even experienced butt pirates like to know what's coming.

Use plenty of lube. Water-based lubes are the safest, at least for women. Oil is bad for vaginal health, so any oil-based lube that could drip down or get pushed in the puss is a bad idea. Silicone lube will make your silicone and some Cyberskin toys tacky, so use it only with toys swathed in latex or made of other materials. While you're fucking, add more lube as needed to reduce friction.

Gem silicone plug.

Beaded Bliss

Follow the same guidelines you would for all other types of anal sex when inserting anal beads. The butt needs plenty of warming up. Make sure your partner is turned on, and her or his butt is relaxed and ready for entry. Caressing the outer pucker with a lubed finger lets the anus know what's coming.

Cover the beads with lube, and then push the first ball in. At first, everything that happens to the butt registers like a tidal wave of sensation, so show respect for the intensity of what your sweetheart may be feeling. Follow her or his lead.

Push in each remaining bead, one at a time, pausing after each to massage the butthole. With an ass full of beads, your lover may be ready for other kinds of sensation. As you bring him or her to a climax, go back to the beads. Ask your lover to tell you when orgasm is imminent, and when it starts, slowly pull the beads straight out through the duration of the orgasm. Don't risk running the string along the delicate tissue of the anus by pulling up or down—draw the beads straight out as you would your dildo or penis. Resist any temptation to pull the beads out quickly; you're not starting a lawn mower. As orgasm floods your lover with pleasure, their anus will thrill to the five distinct pops as the beads come out, one by one.

Any dildo can be used anally or vaginally, but some of them have shapes that are particularly suited for anal play. Smoothness, softness, some of those ripples we keep talking up, and a curve that will angle the dildo toward the prostate or the G-spot are attributes to look for. Use only dildos with flared bases or long handles in the butt, so nothing gets lost up there.

Mistress The Mistress is a long, lean silicone dick we recommend for first-time anal fucking. Its stylized tip resembles the tip of a penis, but its two- to three-finger size is narrow enough for a friendly fit in tight spots. It's supple, so it won't poke tender rectal walls. Its length allows for plenty of in-and-out motion, so the novice can avoid slipping out in the middle of the act. The flared base keeps it from sliding all the way in the receiver's ass and prevents it from popping out of the front of a harness.

Silk Series Silks are truly silky. Made from a firmer silicone recipe, their finish is slick and shiny. Silks have no ridges or bumps that could interfere with the pleasurable rhythm of anal fucking. One of the three sizes available is bound to fit your chosen opening. The smallest in the series is the smallest dildo we carry. For shy, tight puckers, this is a non-intimidating and easy way to test the waters.

Happy endings: Mistress, Silk 1, and Willow.

Willow Willow's gentle curve hugs the curve of the rectum, and aims right for the G-spot and the prostate. The small, smooth Willow was designed specifically for anal sex. It's a popular first-timer's choice because of its size and because it's a bit more bendy than many other dildos. The tip of the Willow is delicately tapered and angled to make that first push of entry smooth and gentle. It's slim and pliant and works as well in a harness as when held by hand.

REWIND! ANAL-PLAY VIDEOS

Sometimes reading about it isn't enough—you have to see it for yourself. Fortunately, there are some instructional videos that can help. Joseph Kramer's unique masturbation video, *Uranus: Self Anal Massage for Men*, invites the sexplorer to enter a world where the butthole is valued, cared for, and celebrated as a sensitive, rewarding part of the body. Although the film is made for men, we think it's inspiring for women as well. It's simply unsurpassed in its non-exploitative appreciation of the anus, and there is no better viewing choice for those who wish to shed their anal shame.

The *Bend Over Boyfriend* videos show women fucking their boyfriends in the ass and sprinkle the "how-to" information throughout. The tapes expose an exciting phenomenon and invite sexually adventurous couples to try it for themselves.

Toys in Babeland's Anal Sex Tip Sheet:
Guidelines for Greatness

USE PLENTY OF LUBE. **The anus and rectum do not produce natural lubrication, so a good lube specifically designed for sexual activity is essential for the enjoyment of anal sex.**

CONCENTRATE ON THE SENSITIVE OUTER RIM AT FIRST. **Having anal sex doesn't have to entail penetration—pressing and rubbing on the outside feels so good, it may be as far as you or your partner want to go.**

CHECK YOUR MANICURE. **File down rough nails—a hangnail can scratch delicate tissue.**

GO IN WITH YOUR FINGER PAD FIRST. **Rather than poking, slowly circle the outside of the anus, then gently push in, toward the front of the body. Ask your lover to bear down slightly, or bear down yourself if you are receiving. When you stop bearing down, the finger will be sucked in slightly.**

USE THE RIGHT EQUIPMENT. **When using toys, always make sure they have a flared base or a string at the end. If you use a toy that slips entirely past the anus and into the rectum, there's a chance you won't be able to get it back out on your own.**

PLIABLE, SMOOTH TOYS **are more comfortable.**

STOP IF THERE IS PAIN, **relax, and try again later.**

CONCERNED ABOUT MESS? **Take a hot shower or bath an hour or two before you have anal sex, and insert a soapy finger in your ass. That cleans you out enough for a shallow visit from your lover's finger or tongue. If you plan to go farther than that, use a simple anal douche to cleanse the rest of your rectum. Or you can plan around your digestion. Remember that you are the best judge of whether it is a good day or a bad day for receiving anal penetration.**

Love yourself no matter what happens!

Every time we host a workshop that includes information about anal sex, a man raises his hand and asks, "How can I get my girlfriend to try this? She did it with someone else, it hurt, and she won't try it with me." Right then the rest of the men nod in somber recognition. Who are these villains giving women bad anal-sex memories, and how can the well-meaning guys with an appetite for anal sex get a fair deal?

We may never know who the culprits are, but certainly justice will find them, most likely in the shape of a "Dear John, You're a lousy lover" letter. It falls to the guys in our workshops to break this dreadful cycle, to explore anal sex with their girlfriends in a manner that leaves the women with sweet memories—and in a willing frame of mind for the next encounter.

Memories of painful sex are some of the hardest to dislodge and put to rest. The ass has the memory of an elephant, which is why good anal sex begets more anal sex and bad anal sex begets no more anal sex at all. Men and women, gay or straight—anyone who has had painful anal sex may be reluctant to try again.

If you have had painful, coerced, or just plain bad anal sex, you may have decided then and there to never attempt it again. Of course, you don't have to do anything you don't want to do. But even if anal sex hurt before, it absolutely doesn't have to again, so if you are willing to consider it or give it another go, be assured that you can take pain out of the equation.

FAQ

Will anal sex give me hemorrhoids?

Anal sex is no more likely to cause hemorrhoids than your daily trip to the john. Hemorrhoids are dilated veins around or in the anus. Anyone who has experienced them knows they cause pain and itching. They come from a variety of causes, some of the most common being sitting down for long periods (like at a desk job), habitually straining to push out bowel movements (often caused by lack of fiber in the diet), and pregnancy.

Healthy anal sex will not lead to the heartbreak of hemorrhoids. If you give your butt what it needs—relaxation, warming up, and lube—you can have all the anal sex you want and never require firsthand knowledge of Preparation H.

Negotiating anal sex with a partner who has had a previously painful encounter with it is not a matter of persuading, cajoling, or trickery. This situation calls for compassion and trustworthiness, which nevertheless may or may not yield the desired results. Despite open communication and good listening, your partner may say no regardless of your promises of a slow, sensual anal seduction.

If you both decide to go ahead, it is important to start slowly, concentrating first on external stimulation before proceeding to penetration. Realize that this could be a long process. Depending on the level of trauma and resistance, external touching may be all the anal attention your partner can handle for some time. All the exhortations to go slow, relax, communicate, and let the penetrated decide what happens go double for this situation. Give your lover room to discover whether a new experience with a new partner can lead to something better than the unpleasant experience in their past.

We are at only the beginning of a time when anal sex is talked about openly and instruction is available in the form of encouraging and factual workshops, books, and videos. We hope more and more people explore anal sex with playful curiousity and don't miss out on the fun.

Try This: Rosebud Massage

The anus is a strong, hard-working band of muscle... and we all know how gratefully tired muscles respond to a rub down. We count on our anuses day in and day out to regulate our digestive traffic. Why not pay your anus back with a well-earned massage? You can do this alone or with a partner.

Massage therapist and Sex Educator Joseph Kramer developed the Rosebud Massage, a technique to dispel tension and to elevate anal consciousness.

● GET NAKED in a room that is warm and comfortable. Have your favorite lube close by.

● START STANDING. Begin to move your pelvis, gently at first, and then more vigorously—thrust and swing and rotate! Kramer calls this "waking the neighborhood." Massage your glutes, the large muscles of your ass, to get the blood flowing there. Really dig in with your fingers.

● LIE DOWN on the bed on your side and relax. Slowly clench and release your asshole. See how slowly you can do it, then see how quickly.

● LUBE YOUR FINGERS: it's time for the rub-down. Place the pad of your finger on the rim of your anus, and explore what your asshole feels like.

● LUBE THE CRACK between your cheeks and slide your hand up and down there.

● WHEN YOU'RE READY, insert a finger and massage the inside of the sphincter by gently stretching it, counteracting its natural clench.

● MASSAGE GENTLY for as long as you like—your ass will appreciate it, whether you opt for an elaborate rub down or just a little quality time—but remember, the more time and energy you put into it, the better the results will be.

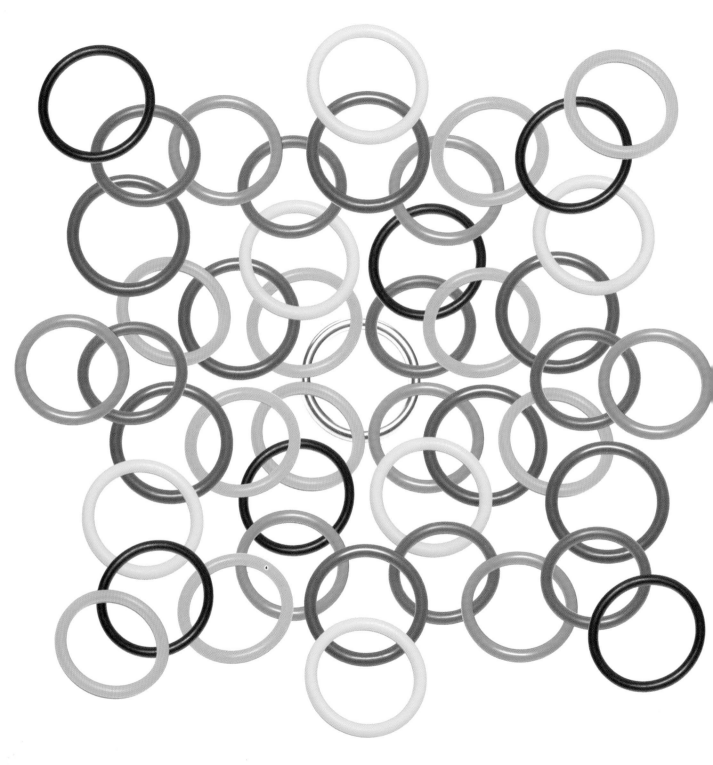

CHAPTER 6

the men's room

Vibrators get women off when nothing else can. But their reputation for heroic deeds in women's bedrooms has overshadowed their other uses, especially for men. One day a man was hovering around our vibrator display, looking as though he needed a translator. We came to his rescue. "This place is just for women, right?" he asked.

No, we explained, men are welcome here, and most of these toys can be used by anyone who feels like giving them a try. We showed him the Double Bullet, a vibrator with two matching bullets controlled by one battery pack. "Take this, for example. This one is perfect for two people of any gender."

He played with one of the bullets, turning the buzzing vibe over in his hands. To our surprise, as he absent-mindedly rubbed the bullet on his nipple, he asked, "But where would a man put this?" We stared at him in disbelief. His body had found a great place to use a vibrator, while his mind still struggled to accept that vibrators had anything to offer him!

toys for boys

Cock rings a-go-go.

Equal Opportunity Toys

It seems as if nearly every day a man will walk into Toys in Babeland, get the lay of the land, look quizzically at a Sex Educator, and ask, "Isn't there anything in here for guys?" Maybe because most of our staff are women and we've created a space where women feel comfortable shopping—with a more boutique-like atmosphere and no explicit sexual images—it throws him off. We hasten to tell these guys that not only do we sell toys for men, and to men, most of the toys we sell can be used by anyone seeking to have a little fun or enhance their sex life.

> Most of the toys we sell can be used by anyone seeking to have a little fun or enhance their sex life.

Getting Off

Most boys start masturbating without any prompting. Though few of us of any gender are truly encouraged in our masturbatory pursuits while growing up, boys' ease of sexual self-discovery is something of an advantage they have over girls. Growing up, boys get an erection to play with, find out instantly how good it feels to touch it, and they're off! It doesn't stop with the basic self-administered handjob, either; everyone has heard of at least a few creative ways that teenage boys have found to get off, from pushing their dicks into a hole cut into a cantaloupe to setting aside an especially soft sock to use for their pleasure. For most guys this masturbatory creativity continues seamlessly through their teen years.

Yet just because men don't need to be taught the basics of masturbation doesn't mean they are loud and proud about their head start. It's no secret that masturbation gets a bad rap in our culture no matter who is doing it. It remains the punch line of countless jokes and is dismissed as the lowest form of sexual expression on the totem pole. Major religions have considered it a sin for centuries. At the start of the nineteenth century, the medical establishment began to treat masturbation as a disease, blaming it for impotence, feeblemindedness, and outright insanity, among other things. Men's natural predilection for jerking off made them particularly vulnerable to the prohibition against it. Inventors applied themselves to this disturbing medical problem, creating devices to prevent people, particularly men, from indulging in this most natural form of sexual expression, lest they drive themselves insane.

> Growing up, boys get an erection to play with, find out instantly how good it feels to touch it, and they're off!

Hot wheels: the Auto Erotic double bullet vibrator.

But when something feels as good as stroking your hard-on to orgasm, there's nothing science or religion can do about it. Masturbation has survived all attempts to curtail or "cure" it, and today it's a healthy part of nearly every man's sex life.

We live in a significantly more permissive time in which most boys and men, though they may

Imagine nipple clamps squeezing sensitive buds, a butt plug filling your ass, or a little vibration on your scrotum

have varying degrees of guilt and shame about the practice, masturbate as a matter of course. But, guys, just because you may be fairly expert masturbators by now doesn't mean you can't benefit from adding a toy or two to your self-loving repertoire. And there are plenty of exciting sensations you have yet to experience. Imagine nipple clamps squeezing sensitive buds, a butt plug filling your ass, or a little vibration on your scrotum—any of these can elevate simple masturbation to new levels.

FAQ

How can I make my penis larger?

We recommend you put aside all thoughts of penis enlargement and work with what you've got. Pervasive sexual shame in our culture sows seeds of fear of inadequacy while stifling open discussions about sex that could alleviate those fears. Usually when guys ask about the best way to enlarge their penises, what they really want to know is how they can better satisfy their lovers, or how they can feel better about themselves sexually. Being a great lover has to do with attentiveness and openness to your own desires and those of your lover. It doesn't hinge on what's between your legs. Be confident in your equipment. You are fine just as you are.

Field Guide to Toys for Boys

Masturbation sleeves, penis pumps, and cock rings—these are the toys built specifically for men's sexual pleasure. Masturbation sleeves and penis pumps add variety to your usual solo fun—picking the toy that feels just right is like treating yourself to the gift that keeps on giving. It's an investment in pleasure.

Masturbation sleeves are also known as "pocket pussies" in sex toy stores that cater exclusively to men. Toys in Babeland avoids masturbation toys that look like women's faces or pussies because we want our stores to be comfortable for women, and nothing shuts a woman down faster than seeing a part of herself rendered in plastic intended to be masturbated on.

When we opened our store in New York and were establishing relationships with our East Coast suppliers, one of our vendors called up to alert us to a product he thought we would want to carry. "Hey, I just got in the most realistic pocket pussies I have ever seen. How many do you want?" We politely declined his offer. Remembering the unusual boutique-like atmosphere of our store, he corrected himself, "Did I say 'pocket pussy'? What I meant was 'high-end vagina.'" Nice try, but no sale. Fortunately, we've found plenty of excellent masturbation sleeves that won't send our female customers running for the door.

Cock rings were originally used to treat impotence by keeping the penis hard, but their medical uses quickly gave way to more recreational ones. Now men use them to get an extra-stiff, supersensitive erection, to stay harder longer, and to dress up for their partners.

While those toys are obviously just for men, vibrators, dildos, butt plugs, and SM gear also have a lot to offer a guy who wants to explore his body and his sexuality. There is no limit to the fun an open-minded guy can have with sex toys.

Expect sublime solo sex with the Fleshlight.

ALONE BUT NOT LONELY: MASTURBATION SLEEVES

Masturbation sleeves are like an upgrade for that favorite old sock. They're made from various soft and pleasing materials, such as jelly rubber, vinyl, or that most flesh-like of materials, Cyberskin. As you may have guessed, they're designed for penetration—they mimic the sensation of fucking.

Fleshlight The Fleshlight is the cream of the Cyberskin-sleeve crop. A big, plastic canister that holds a generous, silky-soft pipe of Cyberskin, the Fleshlight features an opening shaped like a mouth. It looks like an oversized flashlight, so the bashful masturbator can hide it in plain sight. The toy wasn't designed to vibrate, but our astute Sex Educators discovered that the small end of the canister opens to reveal an ideal spot for a bullet-type vibrator. The Cyberskin sleeve is removable for easy cleaning. And as with all Cyberskin, it feels gummy after it's been wet but can be returned to its original silkiness with a dusting of cornstarch.

Blossom Sleeve The Blossom Sleeve is made of jelly rubber, which is slightly firmer than Cyberskin; some men prefer the greater friction it provides. The Blossom's advantages also include being smaller and less expensive than other sleeves. Its inner surface is contoured to replicate the texture and pressure of vaginal walls. From the outside, the sleeve can appear too small for a man's erection, but snugness is the point, and this stretchable sleeve is truly one size that fits all.

Lube is essential for maximum enjoyment of a sleeve. Squirt some right on your penis, into the sleeve, or both, and find a stroke that starts your engine. Although with most toys there is no such thing as too much lube, it may be better to use it somewhat sparingly with a sleeve. One customer reported that the Silver Bullet vibrator in his Cyberskin sleeve shot out the end as he wanked away—so feel free to experiment with amounts of lube until you get it right!

Blossom Sleeve

A penis pump can temporarily make an erection longer and wider, but it cannot permanently enlarge the penis.

PUMP IT UP

Penis pumps are hard-plastic cylinders that fit over the penis and create a vacuum using suction. They are meant to help a man get an erection or to simulate a blowjob. Men use them for the good feeling of the suction or just for the fun of watching their dicks swell inside the tube.

Contrary to the claims on the packaging, penis pumps won't make your penis larger. A penis pump can temporarily make an erection longer and wider, but it cannot permanently enlarge the penis, so don't expect extra girth or length to last past the end of that erection. Dozens of websites sell products that claim to permanently enlarge the penis and therefore improve your life. Some even claim to have workout regimens that build up the tissue of the penis. Don't be fooled—there is no truth to these claims. The extra size you can get from a penis pump goes away with that erection, and the penis is not a muscle, so there is no workout that will enlarge it. A bigger cock will not change your life anyway (unless you want to be a porn star), but getting good at using what you've got is a sure way to make your sex life the best it can be.

Coaxing more blood into the penis enlarges its blood vessels, so the "pumped" erection will feel spongier than your usual one. If you use a penis pump too often or for too long at one sitting, you can damage the tender blood vessels, making future erections softer, so pump with care. If you feel any pain, stop. Never pump for longer than 20 minutes at a time, and no more than a couple of times a week. Enjoy the sucking sensations but don't overextend yourself. A good rule of thumb is to pump until your erection is about its usual size or only slightly bigger.

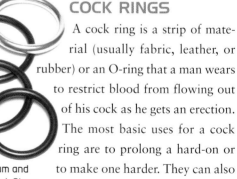

Sweet suction: the Silicone Pump.

The simplest penis pumps consist of a cylinder, open at one end, with the other end connected to a bulb. Other models come with a masturbation sleeve inside the cylinder, and still others are topped off with a vibrator.

The Fireman's Pump is an example of a very simple penis pump. At the open end of its red cylinder, a rubber gasket creates a comfortable seal against the body. The other end of the cylinder has a tube connecting it to a soft, vinyl bulb that when squeezed sucks the air out of the cylinder. The bulb has a quick-release valve to allow air back into the toy.

The Silicone Pump One of our favorites, the Silicone Pump is a clear cylinder lined with a removable, nubbly silicone sleeve. Use a thin coating of lube between the cylinder and your body to create a better seal.

The Penis Pump Our most powerful pump, the Penis Pump's clear, acrylic cylinder comes with a separate brass hand pump. The hand pump connects to a high-quality bicycle-tire gauge that measures air pressure in pounds per square inch (PSI) for precise pumping. The acrylic cylinder's opening rolls out slightly to form a comfortable seal against the body without a gasket. This pump's excellent quality is what makes it an advanced toy—it can create a stronger vacuum than any other pump on the market, so it should be used with extra care.

COCK RINGS

A cock ring is a strip of material (usually fabric, leather, or rubber) or an O-ring that a man wears to restrict blood from flowing out of his cock as he gets an erection. The most basic uses for a cock ring are to prolong a hard-on or to make one harder. They can also be used to attach a vibrator to a penis or dildo for direct clitoral stimulation during penetration. Aside from their functional uses, cock

Aluminum and Rubber Cock Rings

How to Use a Cock Ring

Putting on a basic cock ring is simple—just secure the strip of leather or Velcro in the area between your genitals and the rest of your body. Your cock and balls all go in front. If you are using a seamless O-ring, get a little hard before putting on the ring. First drop one testicle through the ring, then the other, then push your penis through last. As your erection grows and the ring becomes tighter, you may experience a much stiffer and more sensitive hard-on. Some men say cock rings make their orgasms more intense, others can't make it all the way to orgasm with the ring in place. Find out how your body responds by using the Velcro or snap closure—style rings, so you can choose to whip the ring off when you are ready to come.

take the ring off immediately to restore circulation. A cock ring that fits right can be worn with no adverse effects. Some men like to wear them for much longer than the commonly recommended limit of 20 minutes—even through an entire night out dancing. The cock ring keeps the cock semi-hard all night, which makes for a great-looking package in a tight pair of jeans. This kind of long-term wear takes practice, however, and knowledge of your own limits, so play with the ring at home before taking your show on the road.

Stretchy cock rings are versatile, cheap, and easy to put on and take off, so they're good for beginners. You can wear a cock ring the typical way, around the base of your genitals, or place it anywhere along the shaft of the penis for pleasurable pressure. Some models have knobs along the outside rim that can reach the clitoris in certain sex positions, depending on where the ring is placed. Textured cock rings are among the cheapest and simplest toys around, but they provide hours of fun in the sack.

Wearing a cock ring can be a submissive act, and locking cock rings proudly draw out that potential. While they otherwise function in exactly the same way as the more basic models, these include a tiny lock that snaps shut to show that the cock has, for the time being, become someone else's property. Make sure you have the key before fastening the lock.

rings can be decorative as well. Use one to adorn your cock in colorful latex or leather. A cock ring can also be the centerpiece of a trust game; use it bring your dick under a lover's authority. Just like allowing yourself to be tied up, wearing a cock ring can signify your total submission to your lover.

Cock rings function like tourniquets, so it's important to pay attention to the cock that's bound. It shouldn't go cold or numb. If it does,

Rubber Stretch Cock Rings

Can my penis get trapped in that metal cock ring? And what do I do if that happens to me?

Yes, men do sometimes get into a situation in which they'd like to take off a cock ring, but their erection isn't cooperating. That's why it's important that you start with the quick-release Velcro or snap-closure rings, or the rings that stretch. If you do find yourself needing out of a metal cock ring in a hurry, you'll have to lose your erection. Don't panic! Cold water or ice usually shrinks the penis enough to allow escape. Yet you may not have to use the chilly-willy method—if you simply remain calm, stop the action that is keeping you turned on, and lie down and relax, your erection should subside.

Try this one first: the Velcro cock ring.

The Basic Strap This narrow 3/4-inch (2cm) wide, 7-inch (18cm) long, leather or nylon strip with a Velcro or snap closure is the best option for the cock ring newcomer. The Basic Strap allows for an easy escape if you find you are having trouble ejaculating, and you can adjust the fit while you're wearing it. These simple rings can be put on at any time—before you're hard, while you're getting hard, or after you're already hard. Wrap the cock ring between your genitals and your body—your cock and balls all go through the ring. Make it snug but leave room to grow! As your erection gets bigger, the ring will collapse the blood vessels nearest the surface, preventing blood from leaving the penis.

The Dick Kit is a good place to start if you want to play "dress up dick" with a variety of cock rings. It's a sexy patent-leather pouch that comes with a basic cock ring, an O-ring, and strips of leather and

More elaborate styles feature bracelets of leather that stretch the balls away from the body, leaving them deliciously exposed while still delaying ejaculation. Others link together a series of O-rings along the cock, each exerting pressure on the shaft. The number of ball-stretching, shaft-wrapping, clit-tickling, studded, colored, leather, rubber, and plastic cock-and-ball toys is a testament to the appeal of playing with penises.

Erector set: the Dick Kit.

latex, which give you creative control. The longer strips can be laced up and around the cock, used to separate the balls, or just to make a bow to top off your pretty package.

The Deluxe Erection Maker provides a wide array of sensations—and offers the visual thrill of cock and balls bound and vulnerable. The standard leather strap with snap closure encircles the entire genital package. A leather ball stretcher extends down from the strap, pulling the balls away from the cock and forcing them to the bottom of the scrotal sack. A ball separator pushes the testicles apart, stretching the scrotum a little more. There is a tiny D-ring at the bottom of the ball separator for a leash or to clip on weights that will pull the testicles down even farther. Try it if you dare!

VIBRATORS

A man's flesh responds to vibration the same way that a woman's does, which means that a vibrator can bring lots of sexual pleasure into a man's life. In addition to the nipples, vibration feels great on the shaft of the penis, on the testicles, and in and around the ass. Sometimes the joys of vibration can sneak into a man's sex life. If a man's penis is inside a woman, and the woman is

Deluxe Erectionmaker on Ultraskin.

Triple Pleasure on Mr. Big

using a vibrator for clitoral stimulation, the man can receive the benefits of his partner's toy indirectly. This accidental introduction to vibration has brought many a man into our stores looking for a vibrator to call his own.

Men can use most of the vibes that women use. For example, the Wahl Swedish Style massager, the kind that barbers use on their customers' necks, is well suited to a man's needs because it sits on the back of the hand. That prevents the tender flesh of the penis from touching the hard plastic of the vibrator, a sensation many men find uncomfortable. Classic vibes like the Magic Wand and the Slimline are also finding new fans among men. Men frequently use them through a blanket or towel to muffle the vibration, or they place them directly on the perineum, the spot between the scrotum and the anus. There are also a few vibes designed exclusively for men.

The Hugger Vibe A just-for-guys toy that resembles a plastic pansy, the Hugger Vibe has stiff petals meant to flutter on the sensitive tip of the penis. Intense vibration right on the tip of the penis is not every man's favorite sensation, but this vibe pleases those men who seek that direct buzz. The Hugger got its start as an attachment for an electric vibe, but the latest version is battery powered. This vibe also feels great on nipples. Lubricant, our favorite sex product, prevents the petals from pinching.

Orbit Ring Vibe The Orbit Ring Vibe offers a man hands-free vibration on his testicles. A super-stretchy cock ring holds a micro-bullet that can be worn vibrator-down to buzz the balls. This double agent gives a man the pleasures of vibrating scrotum stimulation and goes a long way toward getting the penis and the clitoris on the same pleasure page. When worn vibrator-up, it's positioned to stimulate a woman's clitoris during vaginal penetration—a slow, rocking motion while fucking keeps the vibration on the clit.

Orbit Ring Vibe
on Red Licorice.

BACK THERE

If you've read the preceding chapters in this book, you are already aware of the immense sexual pleasure to be gained from including the ass in sex. Stimulation of the forest of nerve-endings around the anus, the pleasures of opening and closing the sphincters, and the amplification of arousal in the rest of the genitals when the ass is filled with a toy—these gifts of sensation are all there for the taking for men and women alike. While none of the anal toys at Toys in Babeland are strictly for men, there are some that are better than others for sexing up that secret sexual treasure buried in every man's ass: the prostate gland.

Understanding that the prostate is the male G-spot leads many men to do some self-interested shopping in the G-spot aisle at Toys in Babeland. The Crystal Wand, the Cosmic Vibe, and the G-spot attachment for the Magic Wand all double as prostate stimulators. Curved butt plugs aim right for the prostate, while wide plugs press up against it when inside the rectum. Silicone toys are ideal for anal play because they warm up to body temperature quickly and are easy to clean.

The Buddy is a nice, plump gumball of a plug topped by a narrower angled "fingertip" that aims right for the spot—it's a great starter silicone plug. The Tulip Plug is made of supple Cyberskin. It bulges out to greet the prostate, and its multispeed vibration simultaneously relaxes and arouses. It's a joyride for the prostate.

Dildos, especially in the Mistress and the Silk series, are more equal opportunity pleasers. Guys who discover the joys of butt plugs often end up curious about how it might feel to be fucked. A curved, slender dildo with a head, like the Mistress, is great for easy insertion and for stimulating the prostate gland. The Silks are so smooth that sliding them in and out of the ass takes little effort— but works up an erotic charge as the dildo glides across the sensitive flesh.

Fellas, your sexuality is more than just your dick, so don't limit yourself to the toys that were made for it. If you look around and apply your sexual creativity to what you see, the sky is the limit for what you can experience. Men and women are more alike than we are different; so don't be afraid to indulge in vibration, receiving penetration, or anything else you might have considered to be for women only. You have nothing to lose but your hang-ups.

The Multi-Orgasmic Man

The orgasmic mismatch between men and women seems to many like a cruel joke played by the universe— often women are just revving up as their men reach their (sometimes only) orgasmic peak. But what many men don't realize is that they can take control of their sexual energy and experience the whole-body high of orgasm without the deflating effects of ejaculation. Delaying ejaculation prolongs lovemaking, and foregoing ejaculation altogether returns sexual energy to the man's body,

Power to the prostate: Tulip Plug Vibe and the Buddy Butt Plug.

so he can ride his energy to orgasmic peaks several times during one lovemaking session. This is great news for the men who practice this technique, and for their partners!

Most of the sexual self-control techniques come to us from Eastern spiritual traditions. To Westerners, Tantra is the best known. Tantra originated in India around the eighth century B.C.E. as a religion that attended to both spiritual and earthly concerns. Most Westerners think of Tantra as a mysterious and exotic sex practice, but it is actually a spiritual way of life that recognizes that sexuality is a door to the divine, to oneness with the universe. Mantale Chia, author of *The Multi-Orgasmic Man*, describes sexual kung fu as the sexual aspect of Taoism, a philosophy and worldview that originated in China in the sixth century B.C.E. Each of these traditions has its own specific sexual exercises, but their common goal is to utilize sexuality as a path to enlightenment. Whether you wish to study all of the teachings of Tantra or the Tao, or just the part that improves your sexual stamina, developing your sexual capacities is bound to make you feel good about yourself as a lover and as a sexual being.

Though difficult for most people to believe, it's a medical fact that ejaculation and orgasm are separate physical functions in men (just as they are in women). Separating ejaculation from orgasm is the first step in developing the capacity to experience multiple orgasms. Once a guy ejaculates, his erection subsides, and the fucking is finished, at least for a while.

There are several ways for a man to postpone shooting. The testicles start to draw up into the body just before you ejaculate, so gently pulling them back down delays ejaculation. Another method is to apply pressure to the vas deferens, the duct through which sperm is carried out of the testicles, by pressing firmly on the indentation just in front of the anus. Sexual control comes from an understanding of physical energy and how to conserve it. Teachers of Tantra and sexual kung fu recommend practicing these physical techniques to begin to get the hang of reaching orgasm without ejaculating. With some experience, you will start to develop the capacity to prevent ejaculation by redirecting your sexual energy solely with the power of your mind.

Learning to have all of the bliss of orgasm without the deflation of shooting calls for studying your own sexual response, and applying a little discipline to it. Start noticing the range of arousal levels you experience when you are masturbating or having sex with your partner. When you feel as if you are about to come, pull back mentally from that peak arousal and try to feel the sexual energy traveling throughout your body. Clenching your PC muscles just before you feel ejaculation coming on squeezes your prostate gland and delays the expulsive contractions that make you shoot. With a little practice, you can learn to give in to the waves of orgasm without allowing an ejaculation to bring an end to the night.

With all the shame our culture has around sex and pleasure, it's a challenge to open yourself up to slower, deeper sexual experiences, but there are great rewards for the men who do, and for their partners. Men who can sustain their erections past their first orgasm can last as long as they and their partners would like. If a woman likes to fuck, and that's what gets her off, but her sexual response time is slower than yours is (it usually takes women longer to climax), keeping your erection is ideal. Men who practice this technique say they have much more powerful orgasms, and that they feel more emotionally connected to their partners. Devotees of Tantra and Taoism use this type of lovemaking to dissolve the boundaries between themselves and their partners—and ultimately between themselves and the universe.

Zing Ring with Silver Bullet.

Try This: Triple Your Home Runs (Becoming Multi-orgasmic)

1. START SOLO. Extend your masturbating to include your entire body. Caress yourself all over, and delight in how good your skin feels. Breathe deeply and slowly.

2. PAY CLOSE ATTENTION TO YOUR LEVEL OF AROUSAL AS YOU GET TURNED ON. Heat your sexual arousal up slowly until you are ready to ejaculate, then stop ejaculation by either pulling down on your testicles or pushing into the indentation just in front of your anus. Practice this until you can have an orgasm without ejaculating. Once you're accustomed to climaxing without shooting, bring yourself close to orgasm, stop your stroke and squeeze your PC muscles. They contract around the prostate gland and keep ejaculate from getting out. It takes a lot of self-control at first, but with practice you will learn to have an orgasm without ejaculating just by mentally redirecting your sexual energy.

3. BUILD ON YOUR SUCCESSES BY CONTINUING TO PRACTICE. Try pumping your PC muscles at the right moment several times. This disperses your sexual energy throughout your body, readying you for one orgasmic peak after the other.

4. BRING YOURSELF TO ORGASM SEVERAL TIMES WITHOUT EJACULATING, then check in with your energy level. Teachers of this practice say you can expect to feel strong and highly energetic.

5. BRING THIS PRACTICE INTO PARTNER SEX, once you are ready, and treat your lover to your new, more present, slow-burning sexual style.

CHAPTER 7

lube job

It was a humble bottle of lubricant that inspired the creation of Toys in Babeland. One day as we were lounging in Claire's apartment—Rachel resisting going to school and Claire putting off going to work—Rachel spied a bottle of lube on Claire's bedside table.

"You use Slikk?" (The name of the lube has been changed to protect the product's reputation. There's nothing wrong with it beyond its not being our favorite.) "I wouldn't

the importance of being slippery

normally use Slikk, but I got a gift certificate to The Casket" (again, name changed), "and I couldn't find any other way to spend the money. I didn't even recognize anything in there."

It was an affront to our sensibilities that Claire was at a loss for how to spend $10 at the local sex toy store. And in Seattle, a city known for its progressive attitude and its support of innovative ideas! "Why," we asked ourselves, "isn't there a place nearby where we can just stop in and buy the lubes we like? Why?"

That was the spark, the divine inspiration we needed. We decided to open a sex toy store that we would shop in! And for all this, we have lube to thank.

Dive in: there's plenty of lube to go around.

Lubricant is more a sex essential than a sex toy, like olive oil, a staple on the grocery list. It simply makes everything go more smoothly. Sexual lubricant enhances every sexual activity, from masturbation to penetration with a hand, penis, or dildo. Lubricant makes and keeps everything slick. Seen mostly as a supporting character rather than the star of the show, lube is often overlooked by customers with dildos and vibrators dancing in their heads. But lube is not a bit player—it is indispensable for vaginal sex with toys, for anal sex, and for proper use of condoms.

Vaginal lubrication can't be counted on to show up right on cue, just when we want penetration. It's a myth that every woman's natural vaginal lubrication is a reliable indicator of her level of arousal or what she wants. Often a woman is wettest when she first gets turned on, but that wetness can be wiped away or absorbed by toys and condoms long before she's ready to finish fucking. Physiological factors, including menstrual cycle, stage of life, and common medications like antihistamines, can also affect how much and how often a woman gets wet. A bottle of water-based lube by the bed is a simple solution to the problem of desire outlasting natural wetness.

At times, whether through choice or destiny, you might find yourself facing a supersized sex toy or partner. Outsized dildos and large penises glide in far more gracefully with a dollop of lube. Fisting, or inserting an entire hand into a vagina or rectum, is a popular practice for which lube is absolutely essential (as are neatly trimmed fingernails). When only something hefty will satisfy, lube is vital.

Hot and healthy anal penetration of any sort requires lube, because the ass does not produce its own lubrication, aroused or not. Lube is necessary no matter how slender the finger or plug (not to mention cock or dildo!). Satisfying anal sex takes relaxation, communication, and lubrication, and the more of each of these ingredients, the merrier. Lube for anal sex should be thick and plentiful—saliva won't do.

There is no sexual shortcut the ass won't feel and rebel against, so don't skimp! Lubricant reduces friction and acts as padding for the walls of the rectum once the finger, penis, or toy is in.

Safe condom use also requires lube. Latex breaks more easily when it's dry, and latex itself is

> Lube is indispensable for vaginal sex with toys, for anal sex, and for proper use of condoms.

> There is no sexual shortcut the ass won't feel and rebel against, so don't skimp!

absorbent, so lube helps keep the barrier intact. Some condoms come pre-lubricated, with the lube on the outside of the condom, which helps the latex remain elastic. A drop of lube inside the tip of the condom provides further protection from breakage. Men's chief complaint about using condoms is that the barrier diminishes their sensitivity and therefore their pleasure. But that same dab of water-based lube dropped into the tip of the condom before putting it on frees up the head of the penis to slide around and get, within the condom, the friction it craves. Careful though: too much can lead to condom slippage. With this trick, a little dab'll do ya.

Like condoms, many sex toys absorb moisture during ordinary use. If you've never used lube for sex before playing with toys, don't be surprised to find yourself reaching for it now. From the tiniest butt plug to the most daunting of dildos, lube will definitely make playtime with all your sex-toy friends more fun.

Water-based lubes are the best all-around choice. Some people recognize the need for extra slickness during sex, but don't know that a scoop of Crisco or a squeeze of goop from the K-Y tube in the medicine cabinet is not the best option. Household oil, even if it's edible, should never go into a woman's pussy. It takes a while for the vagina to slough off the sticky oil, and in the meantime the oil changes the pH balance of the vagina, encouraging bacteria growth. Oils create a climate for infection. Sexual lubes, however, are hygienic, and far less likely to fix one problem (dryness) while causing another (infection). Another caution: Oil will break down latex condoms. And as for the K-Y? Lubricants designed specifically with sex in mind last longer than jelly lubes produced by the medical industry, which are made to stay slippery only long enough to pop in a rectal thermometer. In recognition of this fact, K-Y recently introduced a lubricant specifically made for sex, not health care. A good lube meant for sex is not a luxury; it's an essential and important ingredient for slick and satisfying sex.

A good lube meant for sex is not a luxury; it's an essential and important ingredient for slick and satisfying sex.

Lube comes in three varieties—water-based, silicone-based, and oil-based. Each has a unique formula, and each has adherents and detractors. Some people are sensitive to certain ingredients; pay attention to your body, and if your privates are itchy or irritated, chances are something in the lube does not agree with you.

Water-based lubricants make up the largest piece of the lube pie. Most water-based lubes contain purified water, glycerin (or another ingredient to add slickness), preservatives, and occasionally artificial flavoring. Glycerin resists evaporation—it's what Hollywood actors used as tears in the "weepies" of the forties and fifties. Those glistening beads of moisture sliding down Barbara Stanwyck's face? That's glycerin. It has what it takes to stay wet under the klieg lights. Once the water portion of the mix starts to evaporate, stickiness follows. But you don't have to reapply lube as it dries—a little mist of water from a spray bottle or a bit of saliva can reinvigorate lube that has lost its slickness.

Many lubes, including Wet Formulas, Astroglide (developed by a NASA scientist), and Forplay, are available at convenience stores. Astroglide is long lasting and lightweight, with the slightly sweet taste characteristic of glycerin-based lubes. Wet is slightly thicker than Astroglide and also a bit cheaper. Forplay offers a thick formula that is nice for anal play.

Sex Grease is a glycerin lube we love (and not just for its supersexy name). This water-based lube is not grease at all, but a cocktail of glycerin and other common lube ingredients, plus vitamins and herbs. We're not sure about the actual health benefits, but it's a nice idea, and the lube smells and feels great.

Glycerin-Free-bies

Basic water-based lubes are made with purified water, long-chain polymers, glycerin, and preservatives. Glycerin and the polymers provide slipperiness. Most women use glycerin lubes with no problem, and enjoy the slightly sweet flavor that glycerin provides, but glycerin is sugary, and sugar feeds yeast. For that reason, glycerin-free lubes have a big fan base among women who are prone to yeast infections. If you find that a glycerin-free lube is irritating, try one with a different type of preservative. The best way to find the lube that suits you is to pick up a variety of little lube samples and compare.

Liquid Silk is a luxuriously creamy white lube with the consistency of lotion. It's pricey but seems to last longer than some of the cheaper lubes, and it gets absorbed nicely into the skin (not right away!), so you're not left with gooey, post-sex stickiness.

Maximus is produced by the same clever folks who make Liquid Silk. It's thicker, clear, and designed especially for anal sex. Maximus has the viscosity of hair gel and provides the cushioning and slickness that anal sex requires. Like Liquid Silk, it doesn't leave a sticky film. Both Liquid Silk and Maximus have a slightly bitter taste that you'll get used to if you love everything else about them.

Slippery Stuff, another glycerin-free lube, has no smell, no color, and no taste. It's also among the least-expensive brands. All these attributes make it a staff favorite. It may not have the staying power of Liquid Silk or Maximus, but it costs much less and can be revived with a spritz of water when it dries out. Interestingly, Slippery Stuff was invented to help scuba divers slip into their wetsuits—but they soon put their wetsuit lube to other uses. Divers do it deeper, after all.

Sensual Power is another glycerin-free lube that our Sex Educators like. It's creamier than most and has a luxurious feel that earned it props from the most discriminating of users.

NATURALS

Among the raft of water-based lubes on the market are some "natural" brands that use either nature's own slippery materials to provide slickness or replace artificial preservatives with natural ones. The natural lubes don't stay wet as long as others, but that's a small price to pay for lube lovers who like to recognize the ingredients on a label. Sylk uses kiwi fruit extract to create slipperiness. O'My uses hemp for its slick ingredient. Probe uses grapefruit seed extract as a preservative.

How to Host a Lube-Testing Event

Intimate or not, your choice—your goal is to compare slickness, stickiness, lasting time, and taste. Get an assortment of different lubes: water-based, silicone, thick, thin, flavored. If it's just you and a lover, the challenge is simply to try them all and remember which one you liked the best. For an unconventional get-together, invite a group of friends over and try the lubes together. We're not suggesting an orgy (though more power to you if that's what you end up with), just an evening with friends in which you get to pass around the lubes, compare and contrast tastes and textures, and share some wisdom. It's a good bachelorette party concept and beats a Botox bash any day.

SILICONE: THE SCIENCE OF SLICKNESS

Silicone lubes last far, far longer than the average sexual encounter, and work with condoms to boot. Nothing in them occurs anywhere in nature; they are an achievement of human ingenuity alone. Many people have taken to silicone lubes the way some of us take to strawberries in winter. A condom-compatible lube that lasts all night? Fantastic! Lube that stays wet in a hot tub? Another benefit of the march of progress! Others remain suspicious of this development, preferring to remain closer to Mother Nature when choosing a lube.

Silicone lube does not get absorbed into the skin. It's composed of molecules larger than those of water, and these molecules skate on top of the skin, creating a layer of slickness second to none. Because it does not contain water, silicone-

Nonoxynol-9

Many water-based lubes contain a detergent called Nonoxynol-9. In the years before Toys in Babeland was a mere glimmer in our eyes, researchers used N-9 to kill both HIV and sperm in laboratory petri dishes and hailed it as an effective tool in the fight against HIV transmission. Later research showed that N-9 could cause microscopic tears in delicate membranes, such as those in the vagina and the anus. These imperceptible cuts facilitate the transmission of viruses and bacteria from one partner to another—so, contrary to earlier recommendations, N-9 may actually increase the chances of disease transmission. Some recent studies have shown that the use of lubes and condoms with N-9 can increase the chance of HIV transmission as much as 50 percent.

In 2001, the U.S. Centers for Disease Control weighed in on this topic, advising people to stop using products with Nonoxynol-9 in them.

Early on, when our women customers reported experiencing what felt like an allergic reaction to their lube, often N-9 was the culprit. When they replaced their lube with one without the detergent, their symptoms would clear up. Most companies that make lubes with this ingredient also make one without, and the ones without are the only ones we recommend. Most condoms come with a little bit of lube on them, so people who know they are sensitive to Nonoxynol-9 should make sure that the condoms they buy exclude it.

based lube virtually never dries out. According to Eros, the manufacturer of the gold standard of silicone lubes, Eros Bodyglide can stay wet in the company's laboratory for up to 10 years. What do you do, then, when you are done being uncommonly slick? Because it isn't water soluble, silicone lube can present a cleanup problem. Warm water and soap works on the skin, but the vagina and anus will stay slick until all the lube is eliminated by natural means. Anally that's not a problem, but the vagina is another matter. Normal digestive elimination will clean the high-tech goo out of your ass, but it's hard to get out of your pussy, which is why many of us are dubious about vaginal use of silicone lubes.

Another caveat for silicone lube: It is incompatible with many silicone toys. The two silicones effect a chemical change, rendering the toy eternally gummy. What would appear to be a match made in heaven is, in fact, a big no-no. Silicone toys' popularity stems partly from their durability and easy cleanup, but once they touch silicone lube some will never be clean again, and that's one big investment down the drain. If you take a shine to both silicone lube and silicone toys, you have to choose between your favorites when you have sex, or carefully use condoms to protect your toys.

Silicone lubes can also do double duty as massage creams. It seems that every day a customer poking around in our massage-oil section will ask whether any of the oils can be used as sexual lubricants. They can't, because oil destroys latex and promotes vaginal infections. And the water-based lubes get too sticky for massage. That's why we keep the massage oils and sex lubes at opposite sides of our stores. Silicone lubes are exceptional in this sense. They are safe for vulval and anal use—and make for a nice, smooth massage. Unlike massage oils that soak into the skin, a silicone lube will stay slippery until it's washed off with warm water and soap.

Eros Bodyglide is a top-of-the-line, silicone-based lubricant. It stays slick through even the longest sex marathon and beyond.

Venus is just like Eros Bodyglide, as far as we can tell, except for the packaging; Venus is clearly marketed toward women.

Eros Water Formulation While on the topic of the mad scientists over at Eros, their Water Formulation uses good ol' glycerin to keep it wet, but even so, some of our friends swear that it is slicker than the rest of the pack, and is ideal for fisting. Eros Water Formulation is also compatible with the silicone toys you may have come to love.

OIL

Oil-based lubricants are tailor-made for male masturbation. As we've already stressed, they're not good for vaginal penetration because oil in the pussy is an open invitation to infection. And oil of any kind destroys latex, so safe condom use with oil-based lube is out of the question. Some Sex Educators accept Crisco and the like for anal penetration with a dildo, but with the plethora of safer lubes on the market there's no need to use oil-based lube for partner sex at all.

FLAVORED LUBE

A few of the big lube companies make flavored lubes in addition to their more conventional products. For those who don't like the naturally occurring flavors of sex, flavored lube can improve the experience of

Erotic Massage

A pair of hers-and-his erotic-massage videos called *Fire in the Valley/Fire on the Mountain* can guide you through a complete erotic massage, including a variety of genital strokes. Keep things slippery with your favorite lube, and spend the evening at home with your sweetie "watching a video."

giving oral sex. But before you rush to mask the taste or smell of your puss, consider that not only is there nothing inherently bad-tasting or smelling about your genitals, scientific studies show that sex pheromones work through our sense of smell to increase arousal. Women's genitals got a wholly undeserved reputation for smelling bad, when in fact the scent is a natural turn-on. (Wonder how that happened?) So forget the insulting jokes you've heard. A healthy vulva has not a trace of fishiness to it. A fishy smell is a symptom of gardnerella, a bacterial overgrowth, which is easily remedied with a prescription gel or a more natural treatment with garlic cloves.

So before you head for the flavored-lube shelf looking to overpower your sweetheart's special sauce, be sure that's what you really want to do. You could end up writing odes to her deliciousness if you give yourself the chance to discover what there is to love. "Your pussy is my morning toast, your juices my butter…" You get the idea.

FAQ

How much lube should I use?

Some folks use lube based on the principle that "you can't have too much of a good thing." Using a handful of lube will certainly keep things wet, but if you don't like the feeling of things being too sloshy, keep it light. Friction is part of the pleasure, so start out with a smallish squirt of lube and add more as you feel it's needed, until you get the right degree of slip for you.

Wet Flavors are sugar-free, which is better for vaginal health than flavored lubes that get their sweetness from sugar. These sugar-free treats come in eight flavors, and are surprisingly tasty. Although colorful, they do not stain sheets. Some people like to use them to improve the taste of a condom-covered dick. Cherry and kiwi-watermelon are the most popular flavors.

Mopping Up

Every brand of lube has its adherents. So while there is no single best kind of lubricant, our advice is to try a few, ask friends for suggestions, and choose a variety (or several) that you like. And whenever you get set for sex, don't forget the lube!

FAQ

How can I improve my natural flavor?

Both women and men vary a lot regarding the taste of their fluids. Stress is a factor, so try not to get too highly strung. Adjustments in diet are the quickest way to effect a flavor change. Munch on fresh fruits and honey, and ease off on coffee, alcohol, spicy foods, and asparagus.

Try This: Slippery Tips

We have no doubt that once you try lube, you'll love it. Lube will become your sex staple. Try these tips to get the most from your lube job:

- KEEP LUBE STASHED IN VARIOUS PLACES, NOT JUST YOUR BEDSIDE DRAWER. Little lube packets make it easy to tuck a single-use size in convenient places, such as your glove compartment, your wallet or purse, your desk at work, your backpack when you go hiking, your spare bedroom...

- IF COLD LUBE DAMPENS YOUR ARDOR, TRY WARMING IT UP BY PLACING THE BOTTLE NEAR A LIGHT BULB FOR A FEW MINUTES. Those who really plan ahead can gently heat the bottle of lube in a pan of hot water on the stove. For last-minute lube applications, apply the cold lube to your hands first, then rub them together—or at least give the lube a moment to warm up before heading south.

- MAINTAIN VAGINAL HEALTH BY KEEPING ANY LUBE THAT'S BEEN UP THE BACKDOOR OUT OF THE PUSS. If you're going for vaginal penetration after anal sex, give a quick wipe down with a towel and start with a fresh squirt.

prisoners of love

Seattle is a very outdoorsy town. We weren't sure how the wall of mostly black leather restraints we call the "Bondage Forest" would be received in a city with such a wholesome reputation. Our fears were allayed one day, however, when in walked a couple who were the epitome of healthy Seattle adventure chic, decked in pile jackets, canvas shorts, and Teva sandals. Rather than heading for the vibrators, as we'd expected, they

bondage and domination

went straight for the wall of black leather. After a few minutes' perusal, they found just what they were looking for—faux fur—lined nylon restraints, in a bright shade of purple. They told us they were river guides who needed bondage gear that was waterproof and easy to spot at the bottom of a duffel bag. Then they headed back out into the Seattle drizzle, geared up for their next adventure, while we vowed never again to stereotype a customer—or a city—by outward appearance.

Hanging around, hoping for a good time: Fuzzy Hand Cuffs, Kookie Restraints, Eye-Spy Blindfold, and Hot Grip clothespins on nylon bondage rope.

From a hapless Batman (in his rubber breastplate) bound and in imminent danger of being sawed in half (tune in tomorrow!) to Angelina Jolie in her *Tomb Raider* catsuit, fetish-y images of bondage and domination are common, even fashionable, in pop culture. Janet Jackson, in her "Live in Hawaii" HBO production, pulled a willing man from the audience and tied him to a star-shaped bondage chair that had been set up onstage. After he was secured, she teased and tantalized him as he sat helplessly bound before her, the audience, and millions of cable-TV viewers.

While legions thrill to media images of vulnerability and aggression, straightforward discussion and acceptance of bondage and domination as healthy sexual desires are, sadly, less common. Although our customers aren't a representative sample of humanity, the sheer number of folks passing through our doors who are clearly intrigued with incorporating some level of bondage into their sex play suggests that "Tie me up!" sings in many a heart.

Bondage and domination sex play consists of erotic encounters in which there is a deliberate exchange of power. For the duration of the encounter (often called a "scene"), the people involved agree that one person (the "top") will be in charge, calling the shots, and dominating, while the other (the "bottom") is willing to take on a more submissive role. The scene could take place just about anywhere there is privacy It could include physical domination, such as being tied up or spanked, or it might employ psychological domination, in which one person gives commands and the other obeys. A typical scene might involve tying your lover spread-eagled to the bed and then slowly bringing him or her to climax. Some people like to create a story line, say, a pirate and a captured prisoner, and to augment the scene with outfits and accents and whatever else makes it more real for them. Other people prefer their costumes to be strictly of the leather/fetish variety and their play to follow the script of strict domme, or dominant master, and willing bottom. At times a scene may include giving and receiving pain, in which case it's called SM, as in sadomasochism (more on that in the next chapter). Many people call all of these kinds of scenes "playing," as in "I really enjoyed playing with you last night." "Play" is an appropriate word, because like a group of kids pretending to be cowboys, SM requires a shared leap of imagination, and like childhood make-believe, it's a lot of fun.

> Bondage and domination sex play consists of erotic encounters in which there is a deliberate exchange of power.

Show him who's boss: the Locking Cock Ring.

People often struggle with their desire to try bondage. But as long as you don't do anything that is nonconsensual or unsafe, there is nothing wrong with trying any kind of sex play that you're curious about. Dr. Gloria G. Brame, author of *Come Hither: A Commonsense Guide to Kinky Sex*, gives five reasons people love bondage: freedom to enjoy sex, adrenaline rush, spiritual journey (she says the restrained person goes deep inside him/herself during the surrender experience), playing with power, and pain receipt/infliction.

The heightened and explicit power exchange of bondage gives pleasure to both partners. For the person being restrained it creates a chance to truly relax into the receiving of attention. After all, there isn't much you can do when bound and tied. In addition to the psychological relief that comes from letting go, the sensual pull of the restraints and the sensation of being helplessly displayed and made available for touch is arousing to many people. Contrary to the reality of being coercively bound, submitting to the desires of a trusted partner or playmate can be a liberating experience—it's freeing not to have any choice!

For the person who prefers being on the other side of the ropes (the top), the rush that comes from having a lover under control is a potent aphrodisiac. Just as the one who gives up control can relax, the one who is taking control indulges in a surge of power and energy. Bondage can focus both partners more sharply into the present moment and intensify the sexual experience in a unique way. These encoun-

FAQ

Am I a sicko for getting turned on by this?

A lot of people who take pleasure in bondage are concerned that they're not normal, but take it from us, a significant proportion of the population gets off on bondage. Power and sex go together like a rainy day and a good book. You can be a happy and emotionally healthy person and still enjoy all the kinky sex you want. Let's just say that you're into something truly unusual. The important question to answer is "Is my behavior safe, sane, and consensual?" *Safe* means no physical harm, *sane* means no psychological harm or weird emotional stuff, and *consensual* means that everyone involved agrees to participate in what's happening. If the answer is yes to all of the above, then go ahead and enjoy yourself.

ters are about consent, about making an erotic agreement, and creating a sensual space together in which each person gets their needs met, whether that need is a thirst for power or a hunger for release.

Bondage is often—but not always—combined with forms of sensation play that would in other contexts be considered painful. All together these activities are called BDSM (for bondage, domination, and

Does fantasizing about being tied up mean I want to be raped?

There is a huge difference between our fantasies and what we would want to happen in the real world outside. Fantasizing about being tied up doesn't mean you want to be raped. Even fantasizing about being raped wouldn't mean that. Some types of fantasies are enjoyable precisely because we *don't* want them to come true, and they offer valuable insight into our erotic maps. Even a fantasy that you really wouldn't want to come true might have elements that you would share in a consensual, trusting, real-world sexual experience. For example, with some advance negotiation you and your lover could figure out a way to "overpower" you that is both safe and sexy.

Negotiation: Getting to Yes, Yes, Yes!

The best way to ensure the success of a bondage scene is to talk it out in detail beforehand. If you have a meeting of the minds (before the meeting of the bodies) about activities and limits first, you'll be more likely to have fun later. Confident that you'll be getting an experience you want, you'll be able to relax and allow it to unfold. If you plan with your partner first, you can come up with a scene that is uniquely suited to both of you. For some people, bondage is a prelude to sex; for others it is satisfying in itself. Some folks love elaborate webs of rope; others want the restraint to be as quick and easy as possible. Sharing fantasies and creating realistic expectations together is the way to get what you want.

SAFETY FIRST

Before any sexual or SM power play, talk to your partner and agree on a menu of sexy activities that turn you both on. If you are playing with someone you don't know that well, make sure a friend knows where you are, whom you are with, and when to expect you back. Never let someone you don't trust tie you up.

Never let someone you don't trust tie you up.

Physical safety in bondage scenes involves making sure that the bonds aren't too tight, any equipment involved is secure, and you have a means of quick release. Even if the bonds aren't tight, hold-

sadomasochism), or just SM, by the people who participate in them. Some regular SM "players" prefer the terms "power exchange" or "sexual magic" to describe their activities. Magic is not too far-fetched a term; good SM play can be enrapturing and transformative. We'll talk more about the sensations and all the great SM gear, such as floggers, clamps, and spankers, in the next chapter.

ing one position for a long time can often cause muscle aches, numbness, and discomfort. The more restrictive the bonds or strained the position, the quicker the scene will become uncomfortable. When experimenting with new bondage positions, limit the pose to 20 minutes or so. Always keep scissors or a knife around for quick release—the unexpected can happen, and trying to untie your spouse while your father-in-law leans on the doorbell or the fire alarm is shrieking has got to rank high on the life-stress test. Medical scissors, which have blunt tips and are angled to slide along flesh, make it easy to snip in a hurry without catching the skin.

The primary physical risks with bondage are that the bonds are so tight they cause damage, or that something dangerous happens while one of the partners is "all tied up" and cannot move. Both situations can be prevented with a little forethought. The rule of thumb when tying bonds is that the top should be able to easily slip one finger (the "pinkie test") between the ropes and the skin of the bottom. Never bind someone with pressure on the joints, such as wrists and ankles, where many nerves and blood vessels travel close to the skin. If the bottom is bound standing up, with ankles or

Panic Snap

FAQ

How can I get my lover to try this without freaking out?

Your sweetie is probably going to take his or her cues from you—if you're tense and worried about the situation, your lover may pick up on your anxiety and run with it. If you want to try a little bondage, just start by telling your lover something along the lines of, "I have this really hot fantasy of us trying some bondage..." Make it sexy, lighthearted, and fun. Be easy and flexible—it might help if you are willing to take on either role. There are lightweight, brightly colored restraints that may be less intimidating to a novice than black leather.

legs tied together, it's very easy for him or her to tip over, and if the arms are bound as well...let's just say a broken nose is a definite scene-ender. Similar disasters may occur if the bottom's legs are tied to an unsecured chair, and in the heat of the moment he or she leans forward. So think before you bind.

If you are bound, and you start to feel numbness, tingling, or pain, tell your partner. But bottoms may become too high on endorphins or too tripped out on pleasing their partner to really pay attention to what is going on physically, so tops should be aware, too—look for any loss of color from the skin, and feel to make sure the skin is still warm. Don't just ask whether everything is okay. Remember, though, that no matter how well you plan, or how magically spontaneous an encounter you are having, tops aren't mind readers (and they get high from playing, too), so if something is hurting or getting numb in a way that's distracting, the bottom needs to let the top know.

If the bottom is tied to a fixed place, make sure that whatever point the rope or cuff is attached to is secure. Save your bottom's pain tolerance for something better than the shower of plaster from a poorly secured eyebolt pulling out of a wall or ceiling.

One of the most important ways of taking care of each other is to agree on a "safe word." That is a word the bottom (or top) can say that means she or he wants to stop playing. If someone uses the safe word, it must be respected. If part of your fun as a bottom is pretending to resist, you

BDSM Safety Suggestions

1. Never allow anyone you don't trust to tie you up.

2. Negotiate the scene in advance.

3. Use a "safe word."

4. Bonds should be snug, not tight.

5. Avoid pressure on wrists and ankles.

6. Check for numbness or changes in skin color and temperature.

7. Don't tie up necks.

8. Keep scissors nearby for quick release.

Gentle but effective: Fuzzy Handcuffs.

can protest all you want and everyone will know you don't mean it, unless you say the safe word. "Red" is a popular choice for a safe word, and some people like "yellow" as shorthand for "please back off a little," without the full stop a "red" would require. If you as the top use anything that prevents the bottom from speaking, be sure to leave him or her with an alternate means of communication in case of a need to stop. If you're gagged, tapping your fingers is a good way to communicate.

Another way to ensure a safe experience is to agree in advance about what will happen in the scene. While the entire encounter need not be scripted, it helps to agree on the central points to a scene. As an example, "I will pretend to be a cop who arrests you for speeding. You may resist arrest, but I will get the upper hand, cuff you, and have my way with you with my billy club. There will be no hitting." Within that sort of agreed upon scene there is a lot of room for improvisation, while the bottom can relax, knowing that nothing unwanted is going to happen. Or try this technique: make lists of things you are or are not willing to do. Such lists can be great springboards for very sexy discussions, even for players who already know each other well as sex partners but haven't explored BDSM yet.

Bondage Basics

The two main types of bondage are sensory deprivation and restraint. Sensory deprivation allows a top to take control of a bottom, and to compel the bottom to focus on his or her other senses, thereby intensifying all sensation. Blindfolding is probably the easiest and most common method of sensory deprivation.

Restraints are for rendering the bottom "helpless." Securing someone's hands and ankles is the heart of bondage. A person whose hands are bound is vulnerable, and if their ankles are bound, too, they can't get away. The quickest, easiest way to bind someone's wrists or ankles is with cuffs made specifically for that purpose. Cuffs can be made from metal, leather, rubber, or nylon. Features to look for when selecting cuffs are safety, comfort, ease of use,

ways to secure the cuffs to other bondage equipment if necessary, and aesthetics. Aesthetics in this case is a fancy word for the "wet test." If just looking at the cuffs makes your cunt clench or your dick thicken, those are the ones you should get. You'll have plenty of choices—there are myriad restraints and truckloads of gear available for those whose erotic imaginations crave the next new thing.

Mini-clothespin

Advance Planning

Bondage scenes are much more fun if the top can move smoothly between activities without a lot of untying and rearranging. So before you start binding, consider what your overall vision is. If you want to have penetrative sex with a female bottom, tying her to a chair won't work. Similarly, tying up your bottom with his or her clothes on could require untying in order to undress, unless you are prepared to tear the clothes off as part of the fun.

A relatively easy and not-too-uncomfortable position in which to tie up your lover for a variety of activities is spread-eagled on the bed. The bed will support both your weights, while much of the bottom's body is deliciously exposed when spread like that. All you need is a feather, an ice cube, or some clothespins, and you're set for the evening.

BLINDFOLDS

If you want to test out blindfolding before buying, try making an impromptu blindfold from a scarf, or you can employ a sleeping mask (another use for that airplane giveaway that you never threw out!). Be advised, however, that while a poorly fitting blindfold may work for catching a few z's on a transatlantic flight, for sex play it's important that the blindfold block out all light. From the bottom's point of view it's very distracting to see even a little sliver of light or a glimpse of the room. For a bottom to really float into the experience of sightlessness, the sensory deprivation must be complete.

Fuzzy Blindfold This toy's decidedly unsevere name describes the lining of faux fur that covers the inside of the large mask. A wide elastic band holds the blindfold securely in place. The fur gently touches the eyelids, but because it's fur, the temptation to open one's eyes is nil. It would be like rubbing your eyeballs on your cat.

Eye-Spy is a sexily styled black leather blindfold with almond-shaped eye patches rimmed with racing stripes of blue or red. The eyepieces are padded, which puts slight pressure on the eyes, again encouraging them to remain closed. A variation on this idea is a blindfold that has as its eyepatches two little discs that thread onto the head strap, allowing adjustment to the exact width of the blindfoldee's eyes. The patches are held in position when the blindfold is fastened.

It's important that the blindfold put only very slight pressure on the eyes, lest the person wearing the blindfold get a headache and end the play date to take some aspirin and a nap.

Trust is a must: the Eye-Spy blindfold.

CUFFS

Leather Cuffs

Leather cuffs are very popular among bondage cognoscenti because they are solid, secure, easy to use, and comfortable. It may seem odd to be considering comfort when the point is to tie someone up and perhaps "torture" them, but it makes sense. The pain that comes from having your circulation cut off and your fingers go numb (along with the threat of permanent nerve damage) is not erotic pain. A bottom who is already physically at his or her limit with overly severe restraint is less likely to enjoy other forms of stimulation, and will have a harder time slipping into an erotic trance-like state of mind.

It's easier to restrain a bottom comfortably with leather cuffs, and the best cuffs are either padded or lined with fur (or faux fur). This lining helps protect the delicate nerves and tendons of wrists and ankles. Cuffs made of thick black latigo leather and lined with soft padding in a contrasting color make for beautiful and effective restraints. Wide bands of leather, which evenly distribute the pressure, are secured with buckles. And the solid grip of nice leather cuffs is compelling enough to induce a submissive state of mind even if the cuffs aren't secured to anything yet. Some leather cuffs come with locking buckles that can be secured with small padlocks, heightening the desired effect; almost all cuffs come with built-on rings to allow for attachment to other restraints.

Ankle cuffs and wrist cuffs can be linked together, or each wrist or ankle can be secured separately to the corner of a bed or to eyebolts in the wall. Wrist cuffs can be clipped to a belt or a collar, or wrist and ankle cuffs can be fastened all four together to "hog tie" the bottom. Most tops use double-snap spring clips or carabiners (like the ones rock climbers use) to secure the cuffs, or else thread ropes through the rings.

Household Hints

Many people have experimented with power play in sex just by holding each other down or getting bossy—instructing a lover to hold perfectly still while "enduring" a tongue bath, for example. When it starts to get serious enough that you want to tie someone up, be cautious in grabbing just any materials at hand. Silk scarves and ties in particular are prone to tightening up more than intended and to create Gordian knots that must be sliced through rather than untied. (Instead of sacrificing that Hermès luxury, invest in some store-bought restraints, even if it's just a hank of rope.) A fun household item that will do in a pinch is plastic wrap. Way back in the 1960s, The Sensuous Woman, by "J.," suggested that women revitalize their marriage beds by greeting their hubbies at the front door decked out in a gown made of Saran Wrap. While we are dubious about that method as a relationship-building strategy, it's a sure thing that plastic wrap can be sexy fun. Tailor it to any outfit that titillates, or coil it around your body to create "Tupperware from hell"—style mummification. It's easy to tear holes in just the right spots, and release is as imminent as the nearest pair of scissors. Don't wrap above the neckline, to avoid impaired breathing, and don't leave the wrapping on too long, lest your bottom "dish," wrapped like yesterday's leftovers, overheat.

Leopard Print Kookie Cuffs

Master Cuffs When only the best is good enough, these sturdy latigo cuffs lined with cushioning foam and covered with a pillow-like layer of soft glove leather are your go-to restraints. The glove-leather lining is available in a sexy bright red or blue, or in basic black. Complete with buckles and D-rings.

Kookie Cuffs These classic thick-leather restraints are made of heavy-duty black leather lined with faux fur and outfitted with stainless-steel buckles and D-rings. The fur cushions the restrainee's joints, and the D-rings provide tie-off points for further restraint.

Nylon Cuffs

For bondage enthusiasts on a budget, nylon cuffs are a quality choice. While they may not be as sensually satisfying as the luxe models, if your main concern is getting the job done on time and within budget, nylon cuffs are just fine.

Bare Cuffs are eye-catching leather cuffs with an unlined, black-leather band topped by a narrower band of contrasting color. Attached D-rings allow for further possibilities.

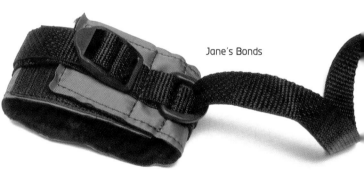

Jane's Bonds

Master Cuffs

Jane's Bonds cuffs are made of durable nylon lined with faux fur. Think mountain-climbing gear. The cuff is secured by means of a nylon tether that wraps around each cuff to the plastic buckle and then extends for another three feet, which makes it easy to tie someone to a tree (or a bedpost) without needing more equipment. As no leather is involved in the making, these cuffs are also a top choice among vegans.

Metal Cuffs and Police Restraints

The good news about metal handcuffs is that they are widely available for less than $20, and are as simple to use as they are easy to afford. Handcuffs work on the principle that as they clasp around the wrist, they tighten and can't be loosened or released without a key. A crucial component of decent handcuffs is a little switch on the side that prevents the cuffs from tightening too much. Cuffs without that safety device are liable to tighten enough to put pressure on the nerves of the wrist, which could lead to permanent damage. The bad news is that even with the safety switch, metal cuffs are more likely to put painful pressure on wrists and ankles—and this is something to very careful about. Never hang or stretch someone by their handcuffs. We don't recommend handcuffs if you can get something better. Metal handcuffs are dangerous, hard, and don't allow for the cuffed to strain against them without risking injury. If you are wearing handcuffs and feel any pinching or numbness, let your top know immediately so that she or he can make an adjustment.

You have the right to remain silent: police-style handcuffs.

Signaling submission with a leather D-ring collar.

If metal is a must-have to make your scene play, try cuffs at the higher price ranges—metal cuffs will increase in heft, in the precision of the locks, and in their severe look. The walls at fetish and other specialty stores groan under the weight of a vast array of historical and futuristic metal fetters.

Thumb cuffs are another option; these tiny cuffs do a surprisingly effective job of keeping someone secured. We hear they work on big toes as well.

COLLARS

Collars are generally of a more symbolic than practical use. They represent ownership, and being "collared" is a sign that one accepts, for the time the collar is worn, the authority of one's partner (now master or mistress). The psychological effect of wearing a collar is profound. Although a collar does not impede breathing, the touch of leather on the throat is suggestive of the power of life and death. Some collars come with rings to which cuffs or leashes can be attached. But if you are leading your bottom around, remember that it's better to pull someone from the front of the collar, to avoid crushing the throat. It is never safe to play with necks, because of the risk of cutting off breath, so be careful.

Princess Collar A narrow band of leather adorned with small metal rivets, this pretty collar is understated but can be symbolically potent if used with the intention to signify submission.

Locking Collar To eliminate any doubt about the meaning of a collar, get one with a lock. Collars built with locking buckles allow the top to secure the collar in place with a small padlock.

Posture Collar The most extreme of collars are built high—any collar wider than two inches (5cm) or so will force the person wearing it to hold her or his head up straight. The strictest of these collars, the Posture Collar covers the entire neck and effectively prevents the bottom from looking down to see his or her own body.

ROPE BONDAGE

Rope bondage is one of the most versatile and enjoyable of SM activities. The snakelike feel of smooth rope pulled across skin, the weight of gathered coils, and the deceptive softness of this inexorable restraint make rope a perfect medium for the practice of bondage magic. While the simple efficiency of leather cuffs and a spring clip meet the basic need of securing a bottom for SM play, rope play can elevate bondage to an end in itself.

Rope comes in a range of colors, sizes, and materials, and it has a long and esoteric erotic history. It feels good against the skin, which is nice for bottoms,

FAQ

I want to be submissive in sex, but not in the rest of my relationship. How can we keep it separate?

One way to handle this is to clearly mark the beginning and end of a scene. A collar is a good signifier. When the collar is in place, so is the dominant-submissive dynamic. When the collar is off, you're back on equal footing.

and when employed by experts it makes for a beautiful presentation. With a little practice, even a beginner can make an elegant and secure knot, while serious rope-bonding divas make bondage as much an art as it is a kinky pleasure.

A simple square knot can secure a bottom's hands at a moment's notice, or a crafty top can weave a spider's web of rope in preparation for an evening date. One customer told us about the elaborate rope body harness that she tied her lover in. "The rope went over his shoulders, between his legs, and around his waist. I tied it so it would hold a butt plug securely in place. Then I had him get dressed in his street clothes and took him to an art opening. No one knew but us—it was a thrilling prelude to an evening of play." Others use rope to fashion their own dildo harnesses. Rope is the most versatile item in any dungeon.

At Toys in Babeland we offer prepackaged 25-foot (7.5m) lengths of bondage rope in assorted colors. You can get it at any hardware store, too—just look for smooth, soft nylon-braid rope, and start tying.

One important reminder: Rope bondage is never for necks.

The raw material of bondage: soft nylon rope.

Boy Scouts, Anyone?

Bondage can be done with simple knots, so start from where you are (you can tie your shoes, right?) and teach yourself as you go along. The Wrap Knot is a clever and secure way to tie someone's wrists or ankles together with a short, spreader bar–type space between them. All you need is a 25-foot (7.5m) length of rope. The bottom's fists should be held about eight inches (20cm) apart. Drape the rope over the wrists so that an equal amount hangs on either side. Bring the ends loosely around the outsides of the wrists again. The loops should lay flat and not pile up on each other. With the last loops, bring the ends up from the bottom to the middle of the length of rope that is stretched between the wrists. Wrap the rope ends over the top of the stretcher and wind it around in opposite directions toward the wrists—it should be a smooth series of smaller loops, no crossing over. Stop 1/2-inch (1cm) from the wrist and tuck the ends under the last loop to cinch the knot. The knot can be tightened or loosened by twisting.

Bondage Furniture

While bondage enthusiasts don't have their own *Wallpaper* magazine (would it be called *Décor de Sade?*), there is an abundance of devices and home furnishings made just for bondage. If you have enough space, consider transforming your basement or spare room into a dungeon. One of the more popular dungeon accessories is the St. Andrew's Cross, a big X to which you can secure someone upright and spread-eagled. Flea market mavens can look for old gynecological exam tables, which are easily adapted to kinky purposes. If you have more modest tastes, a few eyebolts and a stud-finder can help transform an otherwise "vanilla" bedroom in to a bondage boudoir. A simple wood dowel with eyebolts in the end becomes a go-anywhere spreader bar. The Internet is the best place to find pre-fabricated bondage furniture. But if you're handy you can make your own. One bottom we know says it doubles her excitement to make her own equipment. "I love feeling my arm tense up as I'm hammering and sanding, imagining how my bare skin will feel against the wood, and knowing that my efforts will please my top. When I'm tied to it later, I get added satisfaction knowing that I made it myself." Care of the SM soul, we guess.

The Do-it-yourself Dungeon

We're off to Home Depot! A trip to the hardware store offers a number of sexy bondage choices. Solid nylon rope braid is a good bet to start with—if it's bagged, be sure to flex the bag to confirm that the rope is soft and pliable. Get a 100-foot (30m) package of rope, then cut the rope into smaller, more usable lengths. Two 10-foot (3m) lengths, two 25-foot (7.5m) lengths, and one length of 30 feet (9m) are a good ways to divide up the rope. To prevent the rope ends from unraveling, wrap them with electrical tape. Color-code the tape to the length of rope, and you'll always know which one to reach for when you're playing. While at the hardware store, pick up some eyebolts—they can be very handy when converting your boudoir into a dungeon. Get sturdy ones that you can screw into the wall, and be sure to install them securely, so tugging will not yank them out.

Tie Me Up! Tie Me Down!

Think of your bondage scene as contact improv. A few final tips to help you feel secure and keep your scene smooth. Plan the scene with your partner before you start playing. Start with something simple, like a blindfold and light touch. Have a clear beginning and end to the scene, and allow some time for aftercare—cuddling, petting, or just hanging out together as you each settle back into your real-world selves.

Try This: Top or Bottom Quiz

If you want to try SM, but you're not sure whether you'd prefer the top or bottom role, take our quick quiz to see what side suits you best.

AM I A BOTTOM?

I fantasize about being restrained or forced to have sex.

I like to be ravished.

I can't wait for the spanking machine on my birthday.

I would rather respond sexually than take the lead.

I have so much responsibility every day that the idea of "giving it up" is provocative.

AM I A TOP?

I know what I want to happen when I have sex.

I like to be worshipped.

I feel powerful and good when I make my lover hot and bothered.

In childhood games I was the teacher, the cop, or the ringmaster more often than the student, the prisoner, or the circus animal.

I fantasize about my lovers obeying me, and about tying them up or even hurting them.

AM I A SWITCH?

If it all sounds good, or if the first group of statements describes you at some times and the second set at others, you might enjoy both sides of the power dynamic. Known as "switches," players who can take on either role are the most versatile lovers of all.

Bondage Tape makes quick restraints or a groovy outfit.

CHAPTER 9

love me tender (not)

SM sex is as captivating as it is misunderstood. Not all of our customers immediately grasp what floggers and wrist restraints are doing in a bright, inviting sex toy store full of candy-colored dildos and affable-looking vibrators, but it seems as if everyone is curious. As soon as we announce that we are presenting "SM 101," our workshop on the basics of SM, the phone starts ringing, and tickets start flying out the door.

On the night of the presentation, the store is packed with people of every description. The teacher goes through the fundamentals of safety and basic terminology, slowly getting the class comfortable not only with the subject matter but with being in a room full of people, who, like themselves, have SM on their mind. The crowd starts to relax.

playing with sensation

Questions bubble up, such as, "How does the top know when to stop?" and "Where do I go to find other people who are into this?" Almost every time, a student will blurt, "Okay, I really want to do this. How do you suggest I introduce this into my long-term relationship?"

The highlight of the workshop comes when the teacher asks for someone to volunteer to be flogged. It's as if she's asked a roomful of kids, "Who wants to be the first to feed the pony at the petting zoo?" Hands shoot up in an all-out display of enthusiasm—there's no room for self-consciousness when you have a chance to get what you've always wanted.

Thank you, Sir,
may I have another?
A kaleidoscope
of sensation toys

Sex Magic

Soft and sensuous sex feels wonderful, but some of us prefer sex with an edge. Playing with power, intense sensations, and even pain are all elements of sadomasochistic, or SM, sex that can take us to new levels of arousal. What happens during SM sex is not like the violence that erupts from anger or frustration. People who enjoy it aren't driven by animosity, but by desire.

The SM community is populated by tops (those who tie people up, order them around, or administer pain); bottoms (those who take the pain and follow the orders); and switches (they'll do either, depending on the day or who else is at the party). There are parties and conferences, classes, support groups, websites, and magazines. While lots of people enjoy a little slap and tickle without wanting to take on a particular lifestyle or sexual identity, others get a kick out of sharing their kinky desires with lots of potential playmates.

People who enjoy SM aren't driven by animosity, but by desire.

The public SM community is known for its play parties and big scenes that involve more than two people, but many a monogamous couple who confine their sex play to the bedroom like power games, too.

To play properly with pain it is important that you begin by talking with your partner about what will happen before play. For that reason SMers are some of the most communicative lovers around. They explicitly agree to what's going to happen and collaborate in an exchange of power that makes both partners feel elevated.

Safe, Sane, and Consensual

The creed of SM is a tool to protect your partners. "Safe" means guaranteeing physical safety. Any play that could cause permanent damage or a trip to the hospital is not safe. "Sane" means that the players are taking care of themselves and each other emotionally. Working out real-world conflicts or pushing people's emotional limits are not considered "sane" behaviors. "Consensual" means that everyone has agreed to what will happen. Surprises that fall outside the agreed-upon parameters of a scene are not welcome.

Sensational Spectrum

Everyone associates sex with sensation, mostly with skin-on-skin caresses that lead to greater and greater heights of sexual arousal. SM follows the same trajectory, but uses stronger and more intense sensations to create and build connection between lovers.

SM play can involve a variety of different kinds of sensation, through such activities as spanking (very common), paddling, caning, flogging, pinching skin with special clamps, and piercing the skin. These are all popular ways of ratcheting up the intensity of an SM encounter. Clamps or clothespins are used to pinch sensitive tissue. Paddles are used to give a much heavier spanking than your hand can. Canes deliver severe stinging sensations. Floggers pound the flesh like a slapping massage, bringing blood to the surface of the skin, making the flesh hot and sensitive. Just about any implement used to provide punishment or pain outside the SM world can be used for pleasing sexual encounters inside the boundaries of consensual SM play.

A range of sensations: patent leather Star Paddle and Feather Tickler.

Transformation

In general, an SM exchange involves one person making the rules, taking charge, and doling out the sensation, with the other giving up control, submitting to the one in charge, and receiving the sensation. Writer Patrick Califia describes an SM exchange as a liaison in which the top pours energy into the bottom, and the bottom becomes the receptacle for the top's energy. There are a few common ways to create this flow of power. Many SM players borrow situations from real life, taking on roles that have an inherent power imbalance. Perhaps the top plays a doctor giving a physical exam, while the bottom plays the patient who has no idea what they're in for. The power dynamic is clear. Bondage is another common method of getting the energy moving in an SM encounter. Sometimes no setup is necessary. The energy of the top and the energy of the bottom just start flowing.

The tenor of SM exchanges varies widely, depending on the type of scenario the players want. It might be the detached clinical atmosphere of a scientist at work (in this case testing the bottom's limits), or a mating dance of wild animals who snarl and tear at each other as they couple, or a union of spirits inhabiting human bodies as a way of connecting. It can be as simple as two people and a cane or as complex as a staged abduction involving several people that mimics real violence. Any scenario is possible, as long as everyone agrees. In an SM scene, actions that would normally be outrageous violations of decent behavior—everything from hitting and scratching to saying mean things—are allowed. In the context of SM "play," all of these acts—and the feelings they evoke—are transformed.

More bark than bite: leather Spanky slapper.

This transformation is physical, emotional, and psychological. Inside the erotic bubble of an SM scenario, something that might ordinarily hurt—a hard nipple pinch, for example—doesn't, or if it does, it hurts in a way that feels good. Often what happens is that it hurts for a moment, but then the bottom enjoys a flood of endorphins from her or his internal biochemical pharmacy, which turns the sensation into something thrilling. The transformation that turns a nipple pinch into intense feelings of sexual excitement may also be the vehicle that seems to whisk the bottom up and away, like a psychic magic carpet, to a new plane of sexual consciousness. We wish we had a concrete explanation of what happens and why, but feelings this profound are hard to describe. What we can be sure of is that something magic and transformative happens.

If the top and the bottom are connecting well, together they weave a web of sexual energy that creates an intense bubble of rapture. Through domination or administering pain, the top is pouring energy into the bottom, and in taking the pain and giving submission, the bottom completes the circuit. This back-and-forth exchange keeps both people acutely focused in the present moment, and at the same time isolates them in a reality that seems divorced from their real-world circumstances of time and space. Coming down after a really successful and trippy play session feels like coming back to earth after being off in the stratosphere. Even when the scene is not completely transformative in that way, the give and take between partners creates an intense and intimate bond that can make for profoundly memorable sex.

No Pain, No Gain: How to Give and Receive

Developing a good scene takes time; you need the buildup. Most bottoms, no matter how good they are at transforming pain, can't go from 0 to 60 in five seconds. As the top, you must pay close attention to the bottom so that you don't dole out more sensation than your bottom can handle. Processing a sensation takes a few moments. When a

FAQ

I'm confused about why anyone would like pain?

The pain in SM play isn't like the pain from stubbing your toe. In SM, the bottoms use the pain to generate endorphins, to show devotion to their tops, and to test their own limits. The pain isn't an end in itself, but the first element in an alchemical process of transformation.

person is slapped, for example, the nerves fire and send a message to the brain: "Ouch!" The brain processes the information, then sends out a soothing response, and the nerves settle back down. If the person is slapped again before the process is complete, the sensations start to pile up. It's more intense that way—and can become too much. Warming up your bottom slowly gives your playmate time to process the sensations. Sexy talk can also help the bottom move the pain in more erotic ways because it keeps her or him turned on.

As the bottom's brain releases a cocktail of feel-good endorphins, the top can start to turn up the intensity. If you want to go further, moderate both the intensity and the speed of sensation. Joseph Bean, author of *The Flogging Book*, describes the top as continually "seducing consent," that is, giving the bottom just as much but not more than the amount they are willing to take, and then pushing them further and further, without ever crossing that receding line of "too much."

ARC OF A SCENE

An SM scene follows a natural arc that comes from the gradual building up of intensity, which leads the top and the bottom to deeper or sharper levels of consciousness. The scene builds around this intensity between the players. If the power exchange leads to sex and orgasm, it's easy to see how the energy resolves. But sex is not always the climax of SM play. Sex can be the peak of a scene, can take place on the

Going Down

A successful SM session can send a bottom into a state of erotic euphoria. As the sensations build up, be it from the physical or psychological ministrations of the top, the bottom begins to "go down"—to sink into a trancelike state. Welcoming the intensity of sensation, and in communion with the body's responses, the bottom relaxes into the sensation and goes still. The video *The Pain Game*, with Mistress Cleo Dubois, shows a bottom move into a trance state through a competent top's administration of pain.

In the energy exchange of an SM scene, while the bottom is going down into a state of greater calm and willingness, the top is transformed as well. Tops often feel mentally sharper, sense their energy taking up more space in the room, and experience themselves as getting stronger. The energy the bottom gives to the top can make the top seem to crackle with power.

way up or down, or after the pain or bondage is over. Sometimes there is no sex at all. But if orgasm isn't the summit of the scene, what is, and how do people know when it's over?

The best analogy we can think of is a night out dancing—a really fantastic party, where the beats are so good you just stay on the floor for one song after another. As good as it feels, at some point, even if the

Tan her hide: leather and rabbit fur Excytor Paddle.

music is still right on, the energy begins to settle and lessen. The same thing happens with SM. The participants have to be tuned in to each other so that they can ride the wave together. As they come down, feelings of happiness and bliss may wash over them as the real world slowly returns. Colors and smells may seem more vivid in the afterglow, and the players may even feel benevolence toward all of humanity, brought on by the harmonious connection they shared.

SM 101: Getting Started

Trust and communication are the cornerstones of consensual SM play. Before the restraints are clicked shut and the whip sails through the air, each participant must agree to a plan. The agreement should cover both physical and emotional safety as well as include a shared understanding of where the scene will go. It is essential to negotiate beforehand to find areas of common interest and excitement, and to decide how to explore those together.

Once the play date is underway, it's not nice to pull surprises. If you want more spontaneity during the scenario, set up a "Yes, No, Maybe" list before you start. The way it works is that if an activity is on the bottom's "No" list, the top will not do it or even bring it up during a scene. If it's a "Yes," go ahead and do it. For "Maybes," you have to check first and abide by the answer.

With regular lovers negotiations needn't be so formal. As a couple gets to know each other's likes and dislikes, they can play without a lot of discussion. Something new, however, always calls for explicit agreement. It doesn't have to be signed in blood (unless that's part of the fun), but make sure you have consent from everybody. Despite the temptation, don't tie your lover up and then invite your three best friends to the sex party unless you've checked in first.

> Tops, you can't always assume that your bottom will tell you if something is wrong.

Part of the dynamic of SM is that the bottom turns over a lot of responsibility to the top, which means that trust is crucial—especially if the bottom is going to be restrained. The bottom trusts that the top will let the bottom go if asked to, and also that he or she will take care of the bottom while the bottom is incapacitated. The top and bottom each have a responsibility to let each other know if something is wrong. The top should have a means of quick release in case of emergency, and top and bottom should agree on a "safe word" ahead of time—if the bottom says the safe word, the top will stop immediately.

Sometimes bottoms go down into such a deep bottom space that they become oblivious, and may not notice that they are getting cold or going numb from being in the same position too long. The top needs to keep an eye out to make sure that the bottom is doing okay. Tops, you can't always assume that your bottom will tell you if something is wrong. Things to look for are color changes in the skin, cold hands or feet, lips turning blue, or goose bumps.

For obvious reasons, mind-altering substances are not good companions to SM play. Drinking or drug use impairs players' ability to make decisions, the bottom's ability to gauge pain (and thus harm), and the top's attentiveness. Wait until the play is over before you indulge.

TARGET PRACTICE: LOVE TAPS

Percussive sensations like spanking, slapping, and flogging are commonly used forms of playing with sensation in SM circles. Spanking is the lightest and most familiar SM activity. Who hasn't slapped a lover's ass in a moment of spontaneous friskiness as she or he walks past? Spanking is fun because the butt's padded yet muscular constitution makes it such a great target for a slap. It's also the backside of our genitals, and a firm *thwap* on the underside of the butt cheeks sends a wave of sensation right through to our most sensitive parts.

Flogging is among the most popular forms of sensation play in SM. It is a sport and an art form combined—giving a good flogging takes strength and

FAQ

What's the difference between masochism and submission?

Submissives get off on serving and pleasing their dominant partners, whereas masochists are into the high they get from transforming pain into pleasure. You can be both masochistic and submissive, but not all people are. A submissive person may take pain to please a sadistic dominant—but it's the service, not the pain, that blows their skirt up.

grace on the part of the top, and for the bottom, endurance to keep taking the blows. A well-performed flogging scene, with leather tails carving figure eights in the air, is a breathtaking thing to watch.

Most flogging sessions involve a lot of buildup, sometimes progressing not only to harder or faster strokes but to heavier floggers as well. Many people like to use the softer deerskin floggers for warm-up, gently introducing the bottom to the sensation of being flogged while desensitizing the skin. (Wait for a pinkish blush on the skin as the sign to move on to the next level of intensity.) For the bottom, as you get used to a given sensation, it can change from stimulating to boring. Building up the energy by pushing the limits as they recede is the art of SM play.

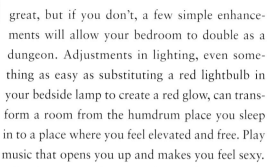

When wielding a flogger or any hitting toy, be sure you know where to aim the blows. Thick, fleshy parts of the body make good targets. Not only does striking thicker flesh protect the spankee from injury, it also feels better. The muscular area of the upper back and the flesh of the ass are the safest places to hit. Never hit someone on the lower back near the kidneys, on joints, or anywhere that nerves, organs, or bones are unprotected. Be aware of differences in body types. While a guy's built-up pectorals may be nice and fleshy, a woman's breasts are not receptive to hard blows.

The delivery of a blow makes a difference, too. If a flogger or other whip overshoots its target and

wraps around the person's side, the force of the blow is greatly increased by the "wrap." Telltale bruises along a bottom's side are the mark of a clumsy top.

The Well-Stocked Dungeon

When starting to explore SM, it's a good idea to plan ahead. One of the things you'll need is a space in which to do your scenes. Just as with any sexual activity, the ambiance of the setting contributes greatly to the overall experience. Set up a space in which you feel relaxed and calm. It should be a sacred place where you give yourself permission to indulge your desires. If you have an entire room to dedicate as a dungeon, that's

great, but if you don't, a few simple enhancements will allow your bedroom to double as a dungeon. Adjustments in lighting, even something as easy as substituting a red lightbulb in your bedside lamp to create a red glow, can transform a room from the humdrum place you sleep in to a place where you feel elevated and free. Play music that opens you up and makes you feel sexy.

Stocking your dungeon doesn't have to cost much. Some nylon rope from the hardware store and a retired wooden spoon from the kitchen make for a good start. Most people who get into SM soon find themselves eyeing different household implements and imagining the sensations they could deliver. A light flogger and a crop are good basics with which to start your official collec-

tion. There is no set list of required toys—anything you find yourself drawn to will probably yield some enjoyment. Like choosing a palette for painting, how you stock your dungeon is entirely up to you. Below are descriptions of toys we like that cover the spectrum of sensation.

TITS UP!

Nipples are such delectable buds of sensation it's no wonder so many great toys exist with which to tease them. The classic toys of "tit torture" (we mean that in the best way) are nipple clamps. Little devices designed to grasp the nipple in an enduring squeeze of pleasurable pressure, nipple

Rubber-coated Hot Grip clothespins

clamps vary in intensity from gentle to savage. For the low-tech players, simple clothespins also work, but the toys we like best are built with some means of adjusting the pressure of the clamp.

Familiar alligator clamps are the standard, adapted for sex play by encasing the teeth in smooth rubber and adding small screws for adjusting the tightness. Serious masochists can remove the rubber tips and get the type that doesn't adjust for maximum grab—but rubber tips are nicer for mere mortals.

When you first apply the clamp, you'll feel a sharp pinch, which shortly settles into a dull ache. That ache can be deceptive. Savvy bottoms know that when the clamp comes off, and blood rushes back into the crushed flesh, that ache will turn into a bolt of exquisite pain. The longer the clamp has been in place the more it will hurt. It's a real mindfuck for a bottom who is afraid of the pain—waiting means postponing suffering, but the longer the clamp's on, the more the release will hurt. Be careful when using clamps so as not to cause more pain than intended.

Clamps can be used anywhere you can grab a flap of skin. The chest and genitals are popular areas, but some people also like to feel the pinch on their back, arms, thighs, or belly. Some diabolical thinker expanded on the clamp to create "zippers" by linking a bunch of clothespins together on a cord. The top applies the clothespins to the bottom, then with one merciless yank pulls all the clothespins flying off. Remember that bit about sensations piling up on one another? The zipper causes a 10-car pileup of sensation and can easily reduce a bottom to screams of agony, followed by a blissful bath of endorphins.

Tweezer Clamps

Tweezer Clamps The most popular clamps at Toys in Babeland are the Tweezer clamps. They look similar to metal tweezers (but are capped with rubber tips) and are attached to each other by a shiny chain.

The intensity of the squeeze is regulated by sliding a small ring up the tweezer's shaft. The closer the ring is to the tips, the tighter the pinch. Tweezer clamps open widely enough to accommodate women's nipples. (Many of the tit clamps out there are made for men's tiny nipples, and women often bust right out of them, if they can even get them on in the first place.)

Butterfly Clamps These have wider jaws that spread the pressure for a more crushing effect. Wide clamps are also good for pinching labia.

ON NEEDLES AND PINS

Tautly bound flesh just begs to be pricked. Sharp, needle-like pricks of the skin can feel like tiny, thrilling electric shocks. These sensations feel especially intense on flesh that has already been warmed up with spanking, slapping, or flogging. All of the toys that deliver these sensations can draw blood, so to be used safely they must never be shared.

Pinwheel One of our all-time favorite sensation toys is the Pinwheel. Appropriated from the doctor's office, where it's used to test nerve response, the Pinwheel has a slim handle ending in a spiny wheel that rolls along the surface of the skin, leaving a trail of tiny pricks in its wake. Applied softly, it will not pierce the skin, but used with a heavy hand it can draw blood. Try it gently on the breasts or genitals,

or more firmly on the back. To really see your lover squirm, run it over the arc of his or her ass. Done lightly it almost tickles. Your lover won't know whether to jiggle with delight or hold very, very still.

Fur Mitt with Spikes For devious tops who like to keep their bottoms guessing, a rabbit-fur mitten with tiny, hidden spikes is a perfect toy. The mitten goes on over the whole hand and is covered with soft, sensuous fur. Loving strokes will make a bottom's eyes glaze over with pleasure. But don't be lulled too far: Small spikes buried in the fur can change that gentle caress into a titillatingly prickly scratch.

Vampire Glove The Vampire Glove is a true top's toy. It's a snug-fitting leather glove with rows of small metal spikes protruding from each finger and from the palm of the glove. The Vampire Glove is also a bottom's delight, because the sensations it produces range from delicious scratching to the meanest pinch you've ever longed for.

THUD AND STING

Hitting implements such as whips, floggers, rods, canes, paddles, and slappers are often described in terms of their "thud" or "sting." If deep, muscle-pounding, solid thunks of sensation attract you, you're probably more of a "thud" person. If it's the whistle of a cane slicing through the air and the white-hot bolt of sensation to follow that excites you, well, then you're a "sting."

Practice Makes Perfect

Want to practice flogging? Hang an old leather jacket on a door or chair, and whip away. The jacket is the stand-in for a person's back, so aim for the shoulders and avoid the lower part of the jacket, which would be the small of the bottom's back. With practice, you can hone your aim while building up physical endurance. You'll be a bottom's dream date in no time.

Floggers

The workhorse staples of many a dungeon, floggers are toys to treasure. The typical flogger has a solid handle about 10 inches (25cm) long that leads to a thick bunch of tails, which are just strips of leather. Often two colors are woven together in the handle. Quality floggers are handmade, and there are artisans renowned for the beauty of their work. Aficionados gather round floggers at parties, comparing their heft and balance as oenophiles might rate a wine. The tails of the flogger can be made from any variety of leather; the most common are cowhide, bullhide, deer suede, and cowsuede. Other floggers are made from latex and rubber, or strands of rope or horsehair. Deerskin is quite soft and entirely without sting. Bull and cowhide are next in order of heaviness. Suede doesn't have the sting of smooth-sided leather. For a particularly vicious leather whip, get one that is oil-tanned. The edges will be thick and crisp and therefore will land with more sting, possibly breaking the skin.

Deerskin Flogger A soft, suede deerskin flogger gives a caress as easily as a beating. A great flogger for warming up, it can be used both for sensual stroking and with more force to give a nice solid thud.

Thudstinger As you might guess, the Thudstinger combines elements of both thud and sting—the inner flails of the flogger are rubber, which is sharp and stingy, but the outside is leather, which is thuddy. With practice you could vary the thud/sting ratio with every stroke.

Bullwhips Classic bullwhips, known as single tails in SM circles, take a lot of practice to learn to use well. Folks who have the training can break the sound barrier—and the skin on a bottom's back—from a distance of 15 feet (4.5m). But if you don't know what you're doing, you could put someone's eye out, or more likely inadvertently hit yourself in the head and feel foolish. Bullwhips for sex play, as opposed to theater props posing as sex toys, are hand-braided and expensive.

Leather Flogger with blue and black lashes and Patent Leather Paddle.

Paddles and Slappers

To give a spanking that won't soon be forgotten, use a paddle. Thick leather paddles with some flexibility have both thud and sting as well as a bit of give, which makes them easier to take. Lightweight leather slappers can offer some of the theater of spanking without the intense sensation of a heavy paddle. Wood paddles are stiff. Score a discarded frat paddle at a garage sale and you can bruise the Greek letters for Deke into your sweetie's butt. Owing to their frequent pop cultural appearances, paddles can seem lighter than they really are. Give the bottom a chance to process the sensation between strokes, or you'll hear the safe word sooner than you might want or expect to.

Spanky Spanky has two flaps of leather about 6 inches (15cm) long and 3 inches (7.5cm) wide. The second flap is cut into strips. As you spank with the uncut side down, the strips from the second layer each slap down on the first. The result is a satisfyingly loud thwack! combined with a relatively mild slap of sensation.

Crops and Canes

Crops and canes dispense with thud altogether and are solely about delivering sharp, stingy sensations. Canes are mean; all the portrayals of errant English schoolboys getting caned on the palm or the bum belie how much damage canes can do. Canes can easily welt skin and cause deep bruising. The tip of the cane travels at the greatest speed, so be careful where that tip ends up. Crops are heavy toys that must be used lightly: Go very slowly and get to know the toy before you swing it hard. The small tip gives a good giddy-up tap, but avoid inadvertently striking with the stiff length of the crop.

COCK-AND-BALL PLAY

While some cringe at cruelty directed toward the most vulnerable part of human anatomy, others find that the thought gives them a warm and tingly glow. Cock-and-ball torture usually involves cock rings that go far beyond the simple devices described in chapter 6. You can tie the whole package up with an elastic lace or leather thong; this has the effect of maintaining or preventing erection, depending on how and when it is tied.

Some men like their dicks tormented with clamps or pinpricks. Cock rings lined with prickles can get the job done while working double duty as erection enhancers. The Pinwheel, Fur Mitt, and Vampire Glove can also be used for prickly dick play. And mini-clothespins can create a dick display that's both aesthetic and agonizing.

Ball stretchers wrap around the scrotum and push the balls down into a taut little knot below the stretcher. They range from an inch (2.5cm) to 2 or more inches (5cm) wide. Parachutes are stiff leather disks that snap into place around the top of the balls. Weights can be suspended from the parachute to drag the balls downward. To many guys the relentless tug is a sweet sensation. The Dick Kit (see page 114) is a good way to get started: It's cock torture arts and crafts.

Hit parade: patent leather Spanky slapper, Riding Crop, and acrylic cane.

FIRE AND ICE

Temperature play is another way to explore SM limits. Ice is straightforward—it's cold! The contrast of ice with warm skin can be deeply erotic. "Fire" can be any sensation of heat, from the dripping of hot wax onto the skin to the slow burn of a heat ointment such as Tiger Balm. If you play with wax, be careful; different types of wax melt at different temperatures. Beeswax melts at a high temperature and can burn or blister skin, so we don't recommend it for wax play. Regular paraffin candles are good, although chemical dyes or scents can affect their melting point.

Before dripping wax on your date, drip it on your own skin so that you'll know just what it is

FAQ

How can I find people to play with?

Most cities have active SM communities, but even if you live in the boonies you can make connections online. SM clubs offer everything from play parties to training sessions on how to play safely. Another possibility is to place or peruse personal ads; be specific about what you are looking for, and don't make your first date with a stranger a play date.

SM Play Tips

- PLAN THE SCENE BEFORE YOU START PLAYING. Negotiate first to ensure you get what you want and that your limits are understood. Be sure to decide on a safe word.

- BUILD UP THE INTENSITY OF SENSATION GRADUALLY. If you carefully warm up your bottom and go slowly, your bottom will be able to take more and go further before the scene comes to an end.

- SWITCH BETWEEN AREAS AND INTENSITIES to vary the experience and give the bottom time to recover. Alternating sensations such as hot and cold or hard and soft keeps it interesting for both of you.

- TALK DIRTY. Maintaining an exciting verbal connection can create a bubble of intimacy between the players that will intensify the experience.

- BE CAREFUL WHERE YOU STRIKE—aim for the fleshy areas of the back and butt.

- AFTER THE SCENE IS OVER, SPEND SOME TIME TOGETHER COMING BACK TO EARTH. This is a good opportunity to indulge in soothing pets, comforting touch, and affectionate talk.

you'll be dishing out. That's a good rule of thumb for other play, too, but it's also extremely easy to do in the moment with wax play. As drops of wax fall through the air they cool down, so the shorter the distance the wax has to fall, the hotter it will be.

Tiger Balm, Ben-Gay, and other heat-based balms can be quite intense when applied to sensitive areas such as the genitals. Go lightly—it takes the ointment five or 10 minutes to reach its full intensity. Never put any oil-based products such as these in the vagina.

Drip Candle With a low melting point, these special SM candles are ideal for sex play, plus they come in a variety of colors and scents, so you can pick the one that's most appealing to you.

After the scene is over, expect to take a little time to adjust back to the regular world. The afterglow can be a nice time to loll around, enjoy some snacks, or just bliss out. (Don't operate heavy machinery!)

This may be a good time to talk. It can be fun just to rehash the scene and revisit the high points. If there wasn't a lot of verbal connection while playing, it feels good to talk over the scene and confirm those really trippy moments with your partner. On the other hand, if things didn't go that well, it might be easier to cuddle quietly and wait to talk about it a little later, rather than while you're still in the moment.

SM skills cannot be learned simply from reading a book. It takes practice. It's never easy to start something new but just as learning to play a musical instrument or speak another language requires practice and patience, so does developing new sexual techniques. We have to be willing to fumble around a little in the beginning of any new pursuit. Bring the same playful willingness to SM that you bring to other new endeavors. Start slowly, and as you gain experience you'll get better at both the communication and the technical skills that good, exciting SM play requires.

You'll find the rewards of your learning period to be well worth the effort.

Toy Care

Thoroughly clean your toys after an SM scene. Toys that break the skin should not be shared. Dedicating a toy to a lover goes a long way in protecting each other from blood-borne diseases such as hepatitis, which can live for a long time on the surface of toys. Maintain your toys by storing them carefully and cleaning them gently when needed.

Try This: Create Your Own Power-Play Scene

Role-play is a good method with which to start experimenting with power and to introduce sensation play into your sex life. Creating a scene in which the power relationship you desire already exists (for example, I'm the president, you're the intern) can ease you into greater exchanges of power. Taking on other identities or roles can also help take you away temporarily from your daily troubles and routine.

The Teacher/Student scene is an easy one for starters. We've all experienced the classroom power dynamic. The teacher sets the rules, and the students either follow them or risk punishment. If you want to take the role of the teacher, you're the top, and command the authority in the scene. If you're the student, you're the bottom, playing the role of the delinquent who broke the rules and is now in for it. As with all SM scenes, it's important to list the possible activities in advance. As the top, you need a road map to know how to indulge your desires within the scene in acceptable ways. For example, say that you're the bottom, and would like a fierce spanking, would like your nipples pinched, and would like to be threatened with but not actually struck by a cane. Once an agreement is reached, the top can start taking on the part of the discipline-happy schoolteacher, and the bottom is free to submit to punishment, with neither of you having to worry about anyone's boundaries being violated.

The teacher might start the improvisation by saying, "You know why I've asked you to stay after class, don't you?" The teacher could then go on to accuse the student of flirting in class, and in that way introduce sexy talk into the scene. Get into it! Following your desire through the scene is the key. Let your imagination go, and see what you find out about yourself.

Star of the show.

CHAPTER 10

keeping it safe

Seattle in the '90s was ground zero in the transformation of coffee from a humble beverage costing 75 cents at the local diner to a high-octane, high-priced lifestyle drink. Stories of common folk making it big by opening a sidewalk coffee cart accompanied a growing awareness of the cultural juggernaut that Starbuck's (with headquarters in Seattle) was becoming. The most popular baristas (the people who make the drinks) were local celebrities who earned more in tips than a first-year corporate lawyer's salary. And we were all caffeine junkies—with overcast skies 250 days a year, who wouldn't want a double latte to shake off the blues?

Meanwhile, AIDS was spreading in Seattle's gay community with no cure in sight. Safe Sex Educators deployed by local AIDS prevention agencies patrolled the bars offering free condoms along with the encouragement to use them. That was a good strategy, but at least one of those educators wanted to find a way to make condoms and safe sex talk an open part of daily life. Taking

safety is fun

her inspiration from the coffee-culture zeitgeist, she created the Condom Cart. In place of the rows of coffee flavorings was a line of jars displaying colorful foil-wrapped condoms and little packs of lube. In lieu of pastries were popular sex toys, including vibrators, dildos, and butt plugs. And instead of the barista there was an informative Sex Educator, eager to support the folks stopping by for free condoms or a chat. What the cart gave to the community wasn't just latex and advice, but a strong message that safe sex was a normal part of everyday life, and that it could be talked about openly and without shame.

It's a Jimmy Hat Jamboree! Remember: safe is sexy.

Sexual Freedom = Sexual Responsibility

We are lucky to live in an era when more sexual options are open to us than ever before, and it's important to learn how to take care of ourselves while living our sexual lives to the fullest. Every sexually active person has to take responsibility for her or his own safety. Even monogamy is not a guarantee. Each encounter requires a clear-headed assessment of the risk involved and the options for safety. For almost every sexually active person—anyone entering a new sexual relationship, anyone with multiple sex partners, anyone who is living with a sexually transmitted disease (STD), or any monogamous couple in which a partner has an STD or hasn't had a clean STD test six months after their prior sex partner—safe sex is a concern.

Despite the seriousness of the issue, safe sex doesn't have to be a mood-killer. Guilt and shame about sex in general can make people passive about taking care of their sexual health, but sex is a healthy part of the human experience, and wanting safe sex conveys both sexual confidence and concern for oneself and one's partner. Familiarity with the tools of safe sex as well as the confidence that safe sex won't make sex clinical make it a lot easier to incorporate healthy safe sex habits into your life. Safe sex can be as highly charged and can feel just as good as unprotected sex.

What Is "Safe Sex?"

Safe sex refers to the precautions we take in order not to contract sexually transmitted diseases.

In addition to AIDS, the most feared STD, there are a number of other viruses and infections that can be passed between partners. Hepatitis, herpes, genital warts, chlamydia, syphilis, and gonorrhea are the most common. The risks of these diseases range from pain to infertility to death, but the sexual transmission of all can be prevented.

Most bodily fluids are kept separate during safe sex. Blood, semen, and vaginal juices are all fluids that can transmit STDs. There are a couple of good ways to minimize contact with these fluids. Engaging in low-risk sexual activity is one method. Dry humping, deep kissing, and mutual masturbation are no-risk

FAQ

I hate the way condoms feel—what if I'm just careful to pull out in time?

Even pre-cum can contain sexually transmitted diseases, and viruses and bacteria can live on your skin, so pulling out is really no protection—not to mention the willpower required. See page 123 for tips on getting better sensation while using condoms.

sex acts. Some people stick to these activities with a new partner while they learn about that partner's sexual history, build trust, and get tested. More commonly, people opt to let the fluids flow, but use appropriate barriers to prevent them from moving from one partner to another.

Condoms, latex gloves, and dental dams are barriers that stop bodily fluids from going where we don't want them to go. New condom and dental-dam designs preserve sexual sensations, making use of the barriers much more pleasurable. Condoms with roomy heads and dams that are thinner, wider, and longer, help make safe sex less of a buzz-kill and a more seamless part of being sexually active.

FAQ

Do lesbians really need to have safe sex?

Yes. There are documented cases of woman-to-woman transmission of AIDS, and diseases such as herpes and genital warts are easily passed between women.

Taking Care of Yourself Is Hot

Sex is deeply personal and our desire for it so strong that talking about it can be difficult. We just want to relax and let the rush of good feelings take over. We fear that if we bring up safe sex with a date, we might jeopardize our chance to have any sex at all. But it helps to negotiate safe sex up front, before that intoxicating rush. If you take care to avoid the risks, you can have uninhibited and pleasurable sex without worrying about disease.

Since the AIDS epidemic, gay men and lesbians have become highly conscious of what safe sex is and how to practice it. It's a life-and-death community issue. Condoms, lube, and dental dams are proudly displayed in many a gay bedroom.

In the straight dating world there is still a stigma attached to showing that you are prepared for sex. Some men claim that having condoms lying around can spook their dates, as if just having the condoms means he intends to use them, no matter what. Many women are still reluctant to carry condoms because they are concerned about being perceived as sluts. But being prepared for safe, hot sex shows confidence, and that's sexy. It's okay to want good sex and to prepare for it. Practicing safer sex shows that you care about yourself and your sex partners. Keeping safer sex supplies near the bed or in your purse is an acknowledgement that you know about the risks involved in sex, you're on top of the situation, and you're ready for action.

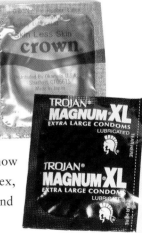

Playing Safe: The Equipment

The bread-and-butter safe sex supplies are condoms, latex gloves, dental dams (or plastic wrap), and lube. Lube is an important accompaniment to the barriers because it keeps them slick and flexible. A supple barrier is less likely to break—and it feels better against the skin.

CONDOMS

Condoms are made from latex, polyurethane, or lambskin. Most are latex, which traps sperm as well as the bacteria and viruses that cause sexually transmitted diseases. There are a huge number of brands of latex condoms, and each one is a little different. Fortunately, they are cheap and widely available in convenience stores and supermarkets, so it's easy to get a variety of condoms to try. One of the biggest problems with condoms, mostly for men, is that they reduce the sensations that make sex feel good. A condom with a good design (and that fits well) is crucial to maximizing sensation, and using it correctly can make the experience more pleasurable.

If you experience condom slippage during sex, or alternatively, you feel constricted, you may need a different size. Condoms come in a variety of sizes and are like shoes regarding fit; just because you usually wear a size 10 doesn't mean every pair in that size will feel good. So shop around until you find one you like best.

Some people find that zippy condom enhancements make them more fun to use. Condoms in pretty colors, glow-in-the-dark, and creatively textured condoms all have their fans. If you're going to wear a raincoat, it might as well be an attractive one! Although the texture on some condoms is usually promoted as being for the pleasure of the receiver, vaginal nerves aren't made to detect tiny bumps, and most anal open-

How to Put On a Condom

It's time to glove your love. Check the expiration date. If the date has passed, use a newer condom. Wait until the penis is erect before putting on the condom. Take care when opening the package, as fingernails and teeth can rip the condom. Tear open the package from the corner with your fingers.

Check to see which way the condom unrolls. Pinch the small pucker in the middle of the disk of the rolled up condom. Squeeze it shut to prevent air bubbles, and hold on to the top inch of the condom while you place the condom on the head of the penis. If the penis is uncircumcised, pull the foreskin back. Unroll the condom down the shaft, squeezing the air out as you go. Air bubbles are a common cause of condom breakage. Be sure to cover the entire length of the shaft to prevent semen from leaking out.

Often the condom is longer than the penis you are putting it on. That leaves a ring of rolled up latex at the base of the penis that does not stretch as easily as unrolled latex, and can constrict the penis. When guys say that all the condoms they have tried are too small for them, this is often the real problem. If you scoot the condom up along the shaft and unroll it completely at the base, you can then scootch it back down, so it's more like a scrunched-up sock than a hard rubber ring, and thus is less restrictive.

ings prefer a smoother ride. Some men, however, find that more texture gives their penis a little extra friction, which can enhance the experience.

Latex allergies are on the rise. Frequent exposure to latex can lead to an allergy or sensitivity that will rule out the use of latex condoms. Polyurethane condoms, which are effective both as birth control and to prevent the passing of sexually transmitted diseases, are available for people who can't use latex. The breakage rate of polyurethane condoms is higher that that of latex because the material is less elastic. Latex condoms are safest, so if you can use them, do, but if you can't, then polyurethane condoms are the next best choice.

Latex condoms are durable, but heat breaks them down, so if you're planning to penetrate your partner for a long time, consider pulling out and putting on a new condom. After ejaculation, don't allow the penis to linger for long in the vagina or anus. As the erection is lost, the condom slips off the penis and come can spill out. While pulling out, hold the base of the condom to keep all the semen in it, and discard the used condom. It's thoughtful to tie off the base so that whoever empties your wastebasket doesn't get your stale splooge on their hands. Condoms can be used only once.

Midnight Desire Condom on a Woody Dildo.

FIELD GUIDE TO CONDOMS

All condoms are not created equal. This guide breaks it down so that you can find the condoms most appealing to you.

Sensitivity

Pleasure Plus condoms leave plenty of room right where the penis is most sensitive—a spot called the frenulum, on the underside of the head. The pouchy  area under the frenulum creates more sensation on this delectable spot by moving back and forth as the penis goes in and out. Though the condom is baggy in this area, it fits snugly over the rest of the shaft, so it doesn't slide off. Pleasure Plus got an A+ in sensitivity from *Men's Health Magazine*. Our customers buy them by the fistful.

Inspiral condoms, designed by the same condom mastermind who invented Pleasure Plus, work on the same principle—extra room where it counts. This condom's tip is built in a spiral shape; it resembles soft-serve ice cream. The idea is that the condom itself ripples over the head of the penis and frenulum as the cock goes in and out.

Kimono Microthin Japanese condoms are known for being extra thin without sacrificing strength. Although they are surprisingly sheer,

Kimono Microthins have a tensile strength and elasticity that keeps them from breaking when many thicker condoms would.

Size Matters

Prime Snugger Fit, Lifestyles Snugger, and Mamba are three condoms that are narrower and  shorter than average condoms. If you find yourself slipping out often, feel as if you are not getting the tight fit you'd like, or have a lot of condom left over at the base of the shaft, try these out for size.

Maxx, Okeido, and Trojan Magnum are for big boys, and have extra length, girth, or both. Trojan  Magnum is the biggest, designed especially for men whose penises are big all over. If condoms strangle your dick even when they are entirely unrolled, try the Trojan Magnum. Maxx condoms are made by the same people who manu-

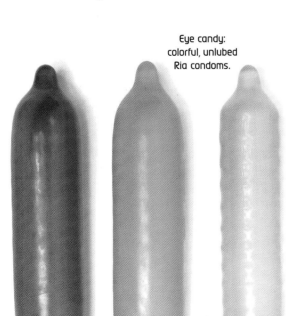
Okeido

facture the Kimono Microthin. Maxx condoms are longer than reg-ular Kimonos and thinner than the Trojans. Okeido is long like Maxx but designed with a pouch at the head. So if you're a man of size, try them each and go with the one that suits you best.

Texture

Trojan Pleasure Mesh Trojan condoms have been around since the 1930s, and the research-and-devel-opment folks at Trojan are coming up with innova-tive designs to this day. The Pleasure Mesh is their latest. Its crisscrossing texture supposedly provides extra stimulation for both partners. There is also an element of dress-up with these—the texturing looks like fishnet stockings.

Kimono Sensation Kimono, a brand known for combining thinness with tensile strength, makes the Sensation, which features bumps inside the condom, for his pleasure.

Unlubed Condoms

Dry condoms allow you to apply the lube of your choice.

Kiss of Mint Tasty and unlubed, these condoms are great for blowjobs because they conceal the taste of latex.

Trustex makes condoms in nicely flavored vanilla and strawberry as well as other flavors.

Ria condoms are thin, come in several colors, and are not lubricated. Rias are inexpensive, so toy users buy these by the handful to keep their vibes, dildos, and plugs clean.

Eye candy: colorful, unlubed Ria condoms.

Polyurethane

Avanti polyurethane condoms are the only brand to look for, as they own the patent for polyurethane condoms. They're a bit pricey, but well worth it if it spares you an allergic reaction on your private parts.

Reality, a.k.a. the female condom, also polyurethane, is made to be worn inside the person receiving penetration. It can be put in ahead of time, and is designed

to give a woman more say regarding condom use. Reality has a small, flexible ring on the closed end, designed to cover the cervix, and a larger ring that remains on the outside of the receiver's body. This condom is versatile, and can be used anally (by both men and women) as well as vaginally. For anal sex, you will need to remove the inner ring. The higher failure rate of Reality is largely due to "user error." Reality condoms don't sheath the penis tightly, so a little more attention is required beyond just putting it on correctly. Make sure the dick goes inside the ring, and doesn't slide in next to the condom. Take care when thrusting to stay inside the Reality.

Lambskin Condoms

The other non-latex option is lambskin. These condoms are not made from lambskin, per se, but lamb intestine. They are less elastic than latex condoms, thus break more often. The pores in lamb intestines are small enough to block sperm, but not HIV, so they only work for pregnancy prevention. Their fans say that these condoms feel great while on, but because they don't protect against HIV, few of our customers use them.

The Right Condom for the (Blow)Job

If the condom is for a blowjob, use an unlubed and possibly flavored condom. The standard lube that many condoms already come greased with tastes pretty foul. Putting a condom on a penis or dildo with your mouth is not a new trick, but it stands the test of time as a sexy way to keep the momentum going. A little practice can improve this technique, too. Someone we know nearly choked on a condom as she was rolling it on with her mouth. Don't let this happen to you! A combination handjob and blowjob works well for getting all the air out of the condom while keeping the cock hard as it rolls on, and for keeping the condom away from your windpipe.

DAMS: PROTECTION FOR EATING PUSSY AND ASS

Sexually transmitted diseases such as herpes can also be transmitted through cunnilingus and rimming. Use of a barrier can prevent exposure to disease as well as to any digestive bacteria.

Latex barriers for oral use are called dental dams. Traditionally, these have been the same dental dams that dentists use to isolate teeth during treatment. Those thick little squares of latex, while available in a number of tastes and colors, were not designed with sex in mind. They are really too small for the job, and are so thick that subtle movements of the tongue, mouth, and pussy are muffled. Into the breach have come Glyde dams—latex swatches made specifically for oral sex.

Glyde Dams Fabulously thin and soft, these large rectangles of latex have a pleasant, silky feel. They

Dam right: Glyde Dams are bigger and thinner than the dams at the dentist's office.

Get Your Licks In: How to Use Barriers for Eating Pussy and Ass

Decide which side is the mouth side, and keep track, as it can get confusing in the heat of the moment. If you do get confused, replace whatever you're using with a fresh barrier (that's where the roll of plastic wrap comes in handy). Lube on the receiver's side helps the barrier slide smoothly so that maximum sensation is transmitted. Hold the dam in place with both hands, and experiment with keeping it taut or letting it hang loosely— each method creates a unique sensation.

are available in cream, black, or lavender, and may be unscented or vanilla flavored. They are so much thinner and larger that they blow regular dental dams out of the water.

Plastic Wrap As fantastic as Glyde dams feel, a perfectly suitable barrier can be found in most kitchens. Regular plastic cling wrap makes for an effective barrier, and it has a lot going for it. It's cheap, convenient, clear (or tinted yet transparent), and thin, and can be torn off in generous sheets. Use regular plastic wrap, but steer clear of the microwavable variety. Microscopic holes in microwavable wrap can't reliably prevent the tiny viruses you're trying to protect against from getting through the barrier.

GLOVES

Latex gloves prevent any cuts or abrasions on your hands from transmitting disease. Finger fucking vaginally and anally are both low-risk activities for the spread of disease, but some people like to use gloves just to be sure—and because they are sexy. The rougher the fuck, or the more fingers (a fist, for example), the greater the risks. Small abrasions on fingers and tiny cuts in the ass or pussy are a risky combination. You may not even be aware of any small cuts because they can be impossible to see. Gloves also cover up dirty hands, which reduces the risk of urethral irritation from sexual activity.

Latex Glove

Gloves used to be big in the dyke community, and plenty of lesbians who came of age early in the AIDS epidemic have a near Pavlovian response to the snap of a latex glove. When choosing your gloves, get the right fit. A baggy glove doesn't feel as good as it could inside the vagina or anus. Look for "powder-free" gloves and consider Nitrile gloves as a non-latex alternative. They are made of synthetic rubber and don't bother latex-sensitive users.

Finger Cots are like the fingers of latex gloves. They are widely used by restaurant workers to cover a finger with a bandage on it, but in the bedroom they're great for covering a finger that is going into an asshole.

Toys and Safer Sex

Dildos, vibrators, and their friends don't ejaculate, but sex toys that are not cleaned after use can still transmit STDs from one person to another. If you are sharing toys, the easiest way to keep them clean is to cover them with condoms before each use. Whisk the condom off the toy, slip a new one in place, and that butt plug can safely pass from ass to ass. Tie the condom off below the base of the plug and it won't slip off. Toys made of silicone can be disinfected between users by boiling for 10 minutes, but other more porous toys are harder to clean. Even if you don't share your toys, women can give themselves a yeast or bacterial infection if they don't keep their toys clean. Hot water and antibacterial soap will do the job, but condoms are quicker. And guys, if you don't clean those masturbation sleeves, you may be safe from STDs, but it's still pretty gross. So wash your toys, or use condoms.

If you've made a commitment to yourself to have safe sex, your decision does not mean that you think your partner has a disease. You can be clear that you treat safety as a basic element of sex. If you are prepared, resolved, and straightforward, then safe sex can happen easily and comfortably. Don't allow sexual energy to drop as you take out your barriers. Keep touching your lover, and keep up the hot talk.

If your partner resists safe sex, explain that it's something you're doing for yourself, and that you can talk about it later. But for right now you just can't wait to fuck/suck/lick (or whatever). Going through each other's sexual histories in the moments before you do the deed in order to decide whether you'll use a barrier or not puts you in a difficult posi-

tion. It's probably easier to set a standard for yourself—"I will have safe sex"—than to try to evaluate someone else in the heat of the moment. People don't always know their health status, and you can't always count on them to tell you even if they do, so play it safe.

As you become more familiar with how to have safe sex, it gets easier. And knowing that you took care of yourself and your partner will make you feel a lot better once the sex glow wears off.

Good sex takes practice. The same goes for integrating safer sex into your sex life. If you practice putting on condoms in the privacy of your own space, you'll be more likely to do it correctly and smoothly when it's time to use them with someone else. So guys, start masturbating, get turned on and do your homework! Women can practice, too—the more comfortable you are with putting on a condom, the easier it will be to use one without feeling awkward. Similarly, think about what you want to say when the time comes to

have sex, so the words will come easily—and you'll be able to come safely.

Make Your Own All-In-One Finger-Fucking, Clitty-Sucking Barrier

1. Get a latex glove that fits well

2. Make a 2½-inch (6cm) slit at each side of the wrist, so that you have made a flap

3. Put the glove on, slit side up

4. Use the gloved fingers for safe penetration

5. Stretch the flap up over her pussy and eat up

RESOURCES

If you want to purchase any of the items featured throughout *Sex Toys 101,* please call 1-800-658-9119, or visit online at *www.babeland.com*

Videos

Betty Dodson, "Celebrating Orgasm," "Selfloving." *www.pacificmediaent.com*
Cléo Dubois, "The Pain Game," "Tie Me Up." *www.sm-arts.com*
Mistress Morgana, "Whipsmart." *www.goodvibes.com*
Carol Queen, "Bend Over Boyfriend," "Bend Over Boyfriend II." *www.sirvideo.com*
Annie Sprinkle, "Sluts and Goddesses: How to Be a Sex Goddess in 101 Easy Steps." *www.gatesofheck.com*

On the Web

www.avn.com Adult Video News
www.bannon.com/kap Kink Aware Professionals, SM-savvy health professionals
www.bettydodson.com the masturbation pioneer's Web site
www.bodyelectric.com a healing arts school in California with workshops nationwide
www.bondage.com how-to articles, advice, reviews, and links
www.cirp.org Circumcision Information and Resource Pages
www.cleansheets.com Clean Sheets Erotica Magazine
www.drducky.com sex educator and web-cam entrepreneur

www.erospirit.org The New School of Erotic Touch
www.fsd-alert.com holistic approaches to women's sexual issues
www.gayhealth.com health information for lesbians, gays, bisexuals, and transsexuals
www.goaskalice.columbia.edu Columbia University's Health Q&A Internet Service
www.hercurve.com a Web community devoted to women's sexuality
www.janesguide.com Jane's Sex Guide reviews other adult sites
www.lesbiansexmafia.org SM support and education groups for women, since 1981
www.libidomag.com Libido: The Journal of Sex and Sensibility, now online only
www.nla-i.com National Leather Association International
www.plannedparenthood.org Planned Parenthood
www.puckerup.com Tristan Taormino's Web site
www.safersex.org features good safer sex facts
www.scarletletters.com an online journal of "femmerotica"
www.sexuality.org Society for Human Sexuality
www.tootallblondes.com Barbara Carellas combines Tantra and SM in New York